SUCCESSFUL BUSINESS WRITING

A PRACTICAL GUIDE FOR THE STUDENT AND PROFESSIONAL

Marion Sitzmann, Ph.D.
Creighton University
Omaha, Nebraska

NATIONAL TEXTBOOK COMPANY • Skokie. Illinois 60077

A special debt of gratitude is owed to the following for their kind suggestions and help in preparing this text: Sue Kamler, Mark Thiesen; David Paolicelli of the Brown Electrical Equipment Co., Carnegie, Penn.; William Henry, President, Rich Lorimer and Fred Mueller of Skinner Macaroni, Omaha, Nebr.; George Wendt of Illinois Association of Professional Insurance Agents; Robert Steele, General Manager of Sioux Bee Corp., Sioux City, Iowa; Chesley Smith of the American Popcorn Company, Sioux City, Iowa; Cathy Campbell of Mutual of Omaha, Omaha, Nebr.; Lynn Harvey; Chris Kleisen; Carl Lo Sasso; and Fr. Robert Halter, O.S.B. This book is dedicated to Fr. Harold McAuliffe, S.J.

890PP 987654321

Foreword

Successful Business Writing is designed to present a thorough treatment of the major forms of business communications: memo, sales call report, business report, letter, and the press release. It is a no-nonsense book that gives the principles and practices of business writing. The exercises at the end of each chapter are intended to make the business student conscious of the world in which he or she will have to operate. The book is intended to prepare the student (within the scope of one semester) for the business world.

The book will prove useful and invaluable to business administration students, those concerned about the techniques of business writing and the business man or business woman who may seek to improve his or her written communicative skills.

Throughout the text, I have taken care to dislodge stereotyped ideas embedded in the minds of students that anyone can write for the business world or that "business writing must of necessity be always dry and dull." The concept I wish to stress throughout the text is that the business world is *alive,* and the good student will capture this vitality in his or her writing. Words like "sensitive," "personalized," "conversational" have been used on purpose in these chapters precisely with the intent of conveying a sense of the "human." The examples at the end of each chapter have a tone of modernity; they are written to express the excitement of the business world to the student in the classroom.

Why is it that there are so few business men and women who excel in business writing? Perhaps I am too simplistic in my judgment to say that they have been turned off by the complicated texts of business writing manuals that have been given to them. The very weight of most of these manuals is enough to make the struggling business student think that the subject of business writing is complicated and, therefore, impossible to learn. This is precisely why the pages of this book have been kept to under one hundred. Theory/example/practice tell it all! If a student thoroughly understands each chapter and does one or two of the assignments, he or she will learn how to write for the business world. Style and precision will come with practice.

Contents

1 Notetaking   1
Effective Notetaking   1
  Organization   1
  Outlining Material   3
Sample Speech   4
Model Outline of Speech by Notetaker   7
Exercises   8

2 Memos   9
Writing an Effective Memo   9
  Conciseness   9
  Completeness   10
  Correctness   11
  Strength   11
Sample Memos   14
  Memo of Instruction   14
  Memo of Request   14
  Memo of Proposal   15
  Memo of Transmittal   15
  Memo of Inquiry   15
Exercises   16

3 Business Letters   17
Purpose of the Business Letter   17
Parts of a Business Letter   18
  Heading   18
  Dateline   18
  Inside Address   18
  Salutation   19
  Body   19
  Complimentary Close   19
  Signature   19
  Stenographic Reference   20
  Envelope Address   20
  Postscript   20
Layout of the Letter   20
  Block Layout   20
  Semiblock Layout   20

Style   22
  Language   22
  Sentences   23
  Paragraphs   23
  Beginnings   24
  Body   24
  Endings   24
Correctness   24
  Neatness   24
  Exactness   25
  Clarity   25
Tone   25
  Positive   25
  Negative   25
  Persuasive   26
Samples of Letters   27
  Inquiry   27
  Refusal   27
  Persuasion   28
  Complaint   29
  Compliment   30
  Information   30
Exercises   31

4 Business Reports   32
General Content and Purpose   32
  Subject   33
  Origin   33
  Frequency   33
  Formality   33
Prewriting Considerations   34
  Analysis of Purpose   34
  Writing for the Reader   34
  Source Materials   35
Organizing the Report   35
  Order of Notes   35
  Revisions   36
  Outline   36
  Order   40
  Headings   41
  Illustrations   42
  Bibliography   46
Qualities of the Well-Written Report   46
  Conciseness, Word Economy, and Completeness   46
  Specific and Concrete Words   46

Sample Business Reports 49
  Short Report 49
  Long Report 52
  Exercises 63

5 Press Releases 64
Traits of a Good Press Release Writer 64
  News Sense 64
  Motivational Awareness 64
Public Relations 64
  The Press Family 64
  Poor Public Relations 65
Writing the Press Release 65
  Inverted Pyramid Structure 65
  Length of Paragraphs and Press Releases 65
  Style 66
  Form 66
  Dates 66
  Omissions 66
Qualities of a Good Picture 67
  Clarity 67
  Size 67
Sending the Pictures 67
Sample Press Releases 68
  George R. Wendt's Press Release 68
  Fr. Matthew E. Creighton's Press Release 69
  The Sue Bee Squeeze Container Press Release 71
  Exercises 71

6 Sales Call Reports 72
Preparation for Writing 72
Material Included 72
  Descriptive Information 72
  Evaluative Information 73
Elements in Writing the Sales Call Report 74
  Judgment 74
  Brevity 74
  Headlines 74
  Objectivity 74
  Exaggeration 74
  Correctness 74
Sample Sales Call Report 75
Exercises 77

Appendix 78

Notetaking 1

Effective Notetaking

Notetaking is personal. There is no universal "right" way to take notes. However, all notetaking involves condensing, organizing, and outlining. When you take notes at a meeting or a conference, you are trying to condense someone else's thoughts into your own words without changing the essential meaning. The key to doing this is to understand precisely what was said and record it correctly with the understanding that you may need to refer to the notes in the future and know just what the ideas they represent were intended to convey. Because it is impossible and usually undesirable to take down word for word what a speaker is saying, an outline may prove most useful to you for recording and then organizing essential ideas. If there is an agenda for a particular meeting, it can help you organize your notes more easily in an outline.

Good notetaking is especially valuable to the manager who has to convey important company decisions and information to his or her subordinates. If the notes are correct, then there can be no doubt as to what an executive wants to have done. Also, notes can be helpful to a manager in answering personal questions or doubts that may arise after an important oral report or an executive speech.

Organization

Order of Delivery

Organization of material is absolutely essential to good notetaking. You should keep together notes that belong together. All notes proper to a section should be kept in that section. The same holds true for notes concerning one topic or one subject. You should use enough words so that, when you return to the notation at a later date, you will be able to understand the significance of a particular phrase or word. Conversely, you should take care to avoid all details that, noted in haste, may detract from or confuse the major points. In a business meeting or in a conference with one's boss, the speaker usually presents ideas backed by examples that make theoretical statements or main ideas relevant and clear. This order of speaking is so commonly used that you may sometimes anticipate the format and take notes accordingly. Example:

   I.   Business has been lagging
      A.   Three factors contribute to a 5% decrease in sales.
         1.   The northeast division has lost two salespeople to competitors.
         2.   Plant No. 5 is working only at 80% capacity.
         3.   Research on a new product is behind schedule.
      B.   Three possible solutions to the problem of decreasing sales need examination.
         1.   Two new salespeople could be hired.
         2.   The machinery in Plant No. 5 could be better maintained.
         3.   More staff may be hired temporarily until research is back on schedule.

This order might be turned around; examples may precede the main ideas. The notetaker needs to pay close attention to the order being used. By presenting examples before the main ideas, the speaker forces the notetaker to decipher what the main ideas are. When this method is used, the notetaker should listen for key words and phrases that flag the main ideas: "Therefore, one can only conclude . . . " or "It is, therefore, quite evident. . . ."

The normal pattern that speakers follow in presenting their ideas is: introduction, main body, and summary. The notetaker should be aware that the item or topics usually will be listed in the introduction. In the second part, or main body, the speaker will cover each important item in detail with examples and factual support. The summary will consist of the most important information, including details highlighting each item. If you, the notetaker, are aware of these three parts of every business speech or conference, then you can anticipate and take notes more efficiently.

Digressions

One of the problems of taking notes is that some speakers wander aimlessly off the topic or digress from the main point. A speaker often gives a hint of going off the track by casually saying, "This reminds me of the time" or "fifteen years ago this happened . . . ." If you, as a notetaker, are aware of how a speaker may digress, you can automatically rest your pen until he or she returns to the main point.

Accuracy

The notes you take must be accurate. Therefore, you must listen carefully to the spoken information. Details such as dates, numbers, and technical terms must be written down immediately during the talk, not reworded or paraphrased later.

Key Words

If you are taking notes on a main idea, you need not slavishly copy down every word. Be selective in taking notes. You should try to determine what are the main ideas of the presentation, along with major examples or pieces of evidence presented to support them.

Techniques of abbreviating words and omitting verbs, adjectives, and adverbs can prove to be very helpful, especially if you are listening to a rapid-fire speaker. If, for instance, the speaker says "The Royal American Tire Company has gone through six years of steady growth," you may simply write: "R.A.T.C. 6 yrs of growth." You must identify key words while the statement is being made, but at the same time you must leave out all excessive information. You won't have time to copy down every word a speaker says. Abbreviation, then, is a necessary timesaving device in business communication. However, be sure to write your notes out fully while the meeting is fresh in your mind.

Body of a Speech

You must identify the main body of the business speech. You will need to take more comprehensive notes on this than on the introduction. You should pay close attention to verbal cues, such as "Let's now cover in detail," or "Let us get down to the key issues . . . ." If the speaker does not clearly announce his or her entrance into the main body, you should be able to detect this when the speaker reiterates point by point the issues mentioned briefly in the introduction.

Summaries

You should pay close attention to the summary or conclusion; it points out the topics that the speaker considers most important. At times, the summary will indicate specific conclusions drawn from the material. The notes you take during a summary should be brief because you have already taken detailed notes on each topic of the main body.

Outlining Material

As pointed out before, recognizing the relationships between bits of information is essential to good notetaking. One of the best ways to indicate these relationships is the outline. In an outline, the main idea of a section will always appear first; details supporting the main idea will be indented. Example:

I.   Business has been lagging.
   A.   Three factors contribute to a 5% decrease in sales.
      1.   The northeast division has lost two salespeople.

Some notetakers may be turned off by the word "outline." Such persons may feel they can be as effective taking notes by simply using an indentation in the outline instead of Roman numerals, capital letters, and Arabic numerals. But the letter and number notation in the outline make it easier to tell the major ideas from the minor ones.

Sample Speech

Farm Strike in 1978

The last time you purchased a steak, did you really stop to consider what you were paying for? Or, what were your reactions when you saw those large parades of tractors, pickups, and trucks motoring down the main streets of the larger cities of this country? What I would like to do today is to give you a few insights or provide you with a few thoughts regarding a large problem within our country.

The plight of the small farmer *is a problem.* When viewing farming or agriculture in this country, we should keep in mind three things. First, the decline in the number of farmers each year; second, the decline in farm prices and the increase in production costs; and third, the decline in the amount of arable farmland each year.

First, I will discuss the decline in the number of farmers each year. Driving through the countryside, one notices fewer farm homes occupied. In 1959, there were 4.1 million farmers in this country. Last year the number had declined to 2.8 million. This is a decline of nearly 50% in less than 18 years.

Along with the decline in the number of farmers is the decline in farm prices and the increase in production costs. Over the past ten years alone, farm production costs have risen from 32 billion dollars annually to 87 billion dollars. In 1976, it was estimated that the cost to the average farmer for producing one bushel of wheat was $5.06. When the farmer took this same bushel of wheat to the market, he received only $2.70. During this past year the figure dropped even farther to $2.40 a bushel.

There is a shrinkage not only in the number of farmers and the prices for their crops, but also in the number of acres of arable farmland each year. Since the beginning of this country, farming has been the main means of making a living and supporting a family. Today farming is one of the biggest businesses in this country. With the advances of the Industrial Revolution, the United States began looking at itself as industrial rather than agricultural; friction between industry and farming began to arise. It is estimated that each year 1.5 million acres of land are lost to urban and industrial development. This is equivalent to a three-mile strip from San Francisco to Washington, D.C.

Now let us take a look at the actual reasons for the farm strike. There are two: (1) the increase of farm production costs and the decrease of farm commodity prices, and (2) the inconsistency of governmental assistance to the farmer.

First, we'll look at farm costs. In 1973–74, the annual net income for an average small farmer was $9,950. Last year that dollar figure declined to $5,300. It's interesting to note that an average person, working 40 hours a week at the minimum wage figure, will earn $5,512 in a year. In other words, the average farmer last year made $200 *less* than the minimum wage. I'd like to use a personal example to further illustrate this point. My father farms approximately 720 acres; his net income for 1977 was $6,000. Analysis shows that this comes to less than $2.00 an hour. An average person working 40 hours a week for a year will work approximately 2,080 hours. My father, however, worked an average of 3,000 to 3,200 hours last year. Therefore, my father worked for $1.80 to $2.00 an hour.

The one thing affecting farm costs the most is inflation. The farmer must pay inflated prices for fuel and farm equipment. For instance, a tractor, the most basic piece of farm machinery, costs as much as $45,000. A truck, the second most necessary item on a farm, could cost another $11,000. The price of farmland, too, is inflated. Around Christmas time, it was necessary for a family near my home to sell their 160-acre farm. It sold for $2,200 an acre. This amounted to well over a quarter of a million dollars. It would be virtually impossible for a farmer within a lifetime to pay off the original purchase price of the land.

The second reason for the farm strike is the inconsistent governmental policy in assisting the farmer. In the early 1930s to the early 1970s, Congress enacted what is known as an "Idle Acre" Incentive Plan. The federal government asked the farmer to leave 10% of his land lie idle in return for a prorated reimbursement for what he would have gotten off the land if he had planted it. In 1973-74, the government stated that there were to be no restrictions on the number of acres planted in crops. The farmer was allowed to plant whatever he wanted, as much as he wanted, and wherever he wanted. From 1975 to the present, the government has restricted the number of acres that could be planted. Congress has tried on numerous occasions to give direct financial aid to the farmer. In September of last year, Congress passed a price-support bill. This bill assured the farmer a certain market price for produce. What is not generally known about this bill, however, is that, of the 13 million dollars allotted for direct payment to the farmers, nine million has already been spent on nonfarm programs such as food stamps and school lunches.

But let us look briefly at the reactions to this farm strike. For the first time since 1932, farmers officially have organized to strike. The movement started in southern Colorado with a group of small-town businessmen and farmers called the American Agriculture. This group stated that, unless the farmers received 100 percent parity by December 14, 1977, the farmers of this country would strike and boycott. Parity is a formula used to measure the buying power of the farmer by comparing farm prices with other prices within the American economy. It is based on the years of 1910-14 because these were the most stable years in the nation's economy. Parity was last adjusted in 1967; it currently stands at 60 percent. Farmers, however, are asking for 100 percent parity, or full reimbursement, for production costs.

Conversely, the nonsupporters of the farm strike say that Congress will never agree to 100 percent parity. If Congress did agree, food prices would rise by 20 percent at the retail market, and inflation plus the cost of living would both rise. The American Farm Bureau (AFB) and the National Farmers' Organization (NFO) cannot support the strike because of antitrust laws. These laws were set up in the early 1900s in order to make it unconstitutional to restrict trade.

One might ask the question at this point: "Why is this farm strike so important?" The answer is simple. The world's population is expected to double within the next 35 years. If the number of farmers and the amount of arable farmland both shrink each year, how can this world population be fed? Our moral objections to reducing the supply of food apply not just to the United States, but to the entire world.

Model Outline of Speech by Notetaker

Introduction

 I. Opening statement
  A. Steak
  B. Tractorcades

Body of Speech

 II. Important factors to be considered
  A. Decline in number of farmers
   1. In 1959 . . . 4.1 million
   2. In 1977 . . . 2.8 million
  B. Decline in farm prices and increase in farm production
   1. In past 10 years from $32 billion to $87 billion
   2. $5.06 to produce a bushel of wheat in 1976
  C. Decline of arable farmland
   1. Industrial vs. agricultural nation
   2. 1.5 million acres lost yearly to roads and industry

 III. Basic reason for strike
  A. Increasing farm costs and decreasing farm prices
  B. Inconsistent government assistance

 IV. Farm costs
  A. Decline of farm income
   1. 1973-74 average net income of $9,950
   2. 1977 average net income of $5,300
  B. Inflation
   1. Energy and fuel costs
   2. Farm equipment costs: tractor up to $45,000 and truck, $11,000
  C. Land inflation
   1. Definition
   2. Example of a neighbor whose farm sold for over $2,000 an acre

 V. Inconsistent federal government intervention
  A. 1930-70 the "Idle Acre" incentive plan
  B. 1973-74 no restrictions on crops planted
  C. 1975 restrictions on crops planted
  D. Direct financial aid by price support
   1. Farm bill misnomer
   2. Of $13 million allotted, $9 million to nonfarm programs: food stamps and school lunches

VI. Impact of strike
   A. Supporters' reaction: 100% parity for crops
   B. Nonsupporters' reaction to farm strike
      1. Claim Congress won't support 100% parity policy
      2. NFO and AFB won't support 100% parity policy

Summary

VII. Why is this an important issue?
   A. World population to double in 35 years
      1. Decline in number of farmers yearly
      2. Decline in amount of arable farmland yearly

Exercises

1. Attend a public lecture and take notes in outline form. Read your notes a week later. Are they clear? Do they cover the main points? Do they include supporting examples and facts? Do you understand your abbreviations?
2. Attend seminar class in the business school and take notes in outline form on what you hear.
3. From a set of outlined notes, write out minutes in complete sentences and paragraph form.
4. Take notes in outline form on a speech that is likely to be reported in depth in a newspaper (a candidate's speech or a presidential address on television). Compare your notes to the news story. Did you leave out any main ideas or supporting examples?
5. (a) Listen to a number of speeches and identify the speakers' clues to the audience to the introduction, the main body, and the summary. What phrases did the speakers use? Did a speaker wander from the main topic? How did he or she begin the digression?
   (b) Make a list of key words and phrases used in an organized speech and learn to recognize them. Remember, efficient note-taking requires good listening habits.

Memos 2

Writing an Effective Memo

A memorandum, or memo, is an informal note to one or more people. Normally, the memo is used for interdepartmental correspondence within a company or organization. It may be written by a colleague to a colleague, a supervisor to a subordinate, or a subordinate to a supervisor. A memo conveys, in writing, important and useful information for the day-to-day operation of a business or organization. It may announce or confirm a meeting, briefly describe a new company policy, or summarize a forthcoming report.

Effective memos combine four elements: (1) conciseness, (2) completeness, (3) correctness, and (4) strength.

Conciseness

A concise memo is one that is brief and clear. Under conciseness, let us examine economy of language, word choice, use of the right jargon, and the use of descriptions.

Economy of Language

The effectiveness of a memo will be in direct proportion to the writer's economy of language. Since time is an important element for any efficiently run company or organization, word economy is absolutely necessary. A simple rule to follow is, don't use five words when one will do. Wordiness has no place in a memo and can often confuse the reader. The simple word can often pack the most punch. Remember, too, a memo should be short. When you write a three-page memo to state a simple message, you are wasting time—yours, the reader's, and the company's. Lack of economy of language can cost businesses millions of dollars and countless hours per year.

Word Choice

Being specific in the choice of words is important. A general statement does not give the reader enough information. For example, "The fabric was good" may have the reader wondering *what* fabric, *what* was *good* about it. The sentence can be improved by stating: "The imported silk had a delicate weave." An effective memo writer chooses simple and exact words because clear and quick action cannot be undertaken if the memo is not understood. Example: "The conflagration of Building 3 will necessitate the fabrication of a new structure." This sentence could be better worded: "Building 3 will have to be rebuilt because of fire."

Use of the Right Jargon

Words used in the memo should be appropriate to the reader's outlook and interests. Each vocation has its own special jargon. Consequently, in order to communicate successfully with persons of other professions, the memo writer must be a master of *vocabularies,* not of a single vocabulary. For example, doctors, lawyers, carpenters, and plumbers all use special vocabularies; their memos to one another often mean nothing to those outside their calling. By using the correct technical word, the memo writer can avoid confusion and misinterpretation.

Use of Descriptions

Certain descriptions are useful in memo writing; these are the psychological tools that allow the reader to see, hear, enjoy, and profit from the words. For example, memos exchanged between buyers and sellers of clothing might include elaborate descriptions of the texture or "feel" of a certain type of cloth; all these details are extremely important in business negotiations. Example: "The Cartier Collection of suits has flattering designer details such as the bowed lapels. Meticulously tailored, these 45% worsted wool suits have a soft, textured weave featuring a bright sheen finish." To a buyer or seller of clothing, these descriptions increase the effectiveness of the memo.

Completeness

Format

All memos must include a subject heading, receiver's name or distribution list, date, and sender's name. The subject heading indicates what is discussed in the memo. If the memo is not to be filed and if the sender works with the receiver, then the first name, nickname, or even initials may be used. The date is essential on all memos for reference purposes and to avoid confusion.

Anticipating Misunderstanding

Before writing the memo, the sender should anticipate possible misunderstandings by asking himself or herself pertinent questions. Who am

I writing to? (You would not write in the same style to your boss that you would to a coworker.) What is the message? The five Ws and an H (who, what, when, where, why, and how) are useful questions in being sure that the memo is clearly understood.

Correctness

Accuracy of Facts, Grammar, and Spelling

One should check and recheck all facts, grammar, and spelling; a mistake indicates carelessness and can irritate the receiver. Accuracy makes you, the writer, believable to the reader.

Verbal Intelligence

One should make sure that the words used mean precisely what the sender thinks they mean. What is fact should clearly be distinguished from opinion.

Neatness and Organization

Attractive appearance can make a favorable impression on the reader. Faint print may give the impression that the sender is not careful and neat. The correctness and neatness of the typing are sometimes as vital to the success of the message as the central idea. A neat, well-organized, well-written memo is likely to get a faster, more positive response than one that is messy and hard to read.

Strength

Tone

Graciousness and sincerity are the hallmark of a good memo writer. Often, the tone of a memo is affected by the writer's state of mind at the time of writing. One should never write and send a memo when irritated, upset, or disturbed. The result may be a return memo "in kind." The receiver cannot be expected to know that the sender was upset about a traffic ticket when the memo was written. A neutral tone should also be avoided since it is too mechanical and emotionless. The overall tone should be courteous. More beneficial action will result from a memo that is courteous than from one that is sarcastic, complaining, or demanding. Example: "Despite the heavy daily work load in the Purchasing Department, I will accept the appointment as an advisor to our firm's Employee Credit Bureau." A more positive tone might be: "Please add my name to the advisor's list of the firm's Employee Credit Bureau, and let me know when I may start and how I may help." The time it takes to write a considerate, pleasant memo will be paid off in a good work relationship with the receiver.

Tact

"Chip-on-the-shoulder thought" can grate on the nerves of others who are sensitive to the psychological tone of a memo. Example: "I thought that all our employees were required to have at least a high school diploma. I can see that some people on your staff can't understand basic orders, etc." The attitude should be that the sender "has" something for the reader rather than that the sender "wants" something from the reader. A positive attitude is usually the most effective; it is always dependable, constructive, and cooperative. A negative attitude, although sometimes necessary, can be dangerous, destructive, and antagonistic. Example:

"This is in reply to your memo of June 3, 19__, in which you inquired why something hasn't been done about the broken air-conditioning unit in Room 4-B. To date, the repair company that we usually do business with is out on strike. As soon as the strike is over, I am sure that the air-conditioning unit will be fixed. In the meantime, I would suggest that instead of wearing the formal shirt, tie, and coat which is required of all our employees . . . you wear very light summer clothing."

A more positive tone is established by the following:

"The air-conditioning unit in 4-B will be repaired in the very near future. The repair company that we do business with has informed us that they are now on strike. Another repair company has been contacted; the air-conditioning unit in 4-B *will be* fixed in two days."

In this regard, the sage advice from the fourth century of C. Julius Victor (maybe one of the first memo writers) might be helpful: "One should write as if the receiver were actually present." If the writer must state something contrary to the reader's opinions, he or she might preface an unfavorable comment by a tactful statement. For example: "Even though all suggestions were considered seriously, the final decision is . . . " or "Having studied a record of your previous employment, a recent review of our plant's demands for the forthcoming year leads to the realistic conclusion that no new personnel . . . . "

Style

Probably the most effective style in writing memos is the "talk approach." This method, which is natural and similar to conversation, helps the writer to avoid stilted and artificial language, as in the following example.

"I was delighted to approve your request during our long-distance phone call on Tuesday. Your description of the new publicity on the condominiums at Lake Shasta will affect in a positive way the sensibilities of potential purchasers. I shall deliberate on these matters with you when I come to your office on July 5, at 10:00 a.m."

One way to avoid such artificial language is to begin writing as soon as you know precisely what you are going to say; otherwise, the style may become too formal and studied. Before the final writing, you should review the ideas you want to convey, be sure that the tone is appropriate, check for a natural, conversational style, and consider how the reader is likely to react to the memo. Also, in writing a business memo, it is helpful to visualize the reader's surroundings and associates at the time he or she will be reading the memo. The total context must be considered! This is especially true if the memo involves some point of correction or criticism.

Placement of Words

The beginning and ending of sentences can attract the reader's attention. The position of a verb or noun in a sentence can make a strong statement from a weak one. Here is an example of weak positioning of words: "One way of making sure the words in a memo are spelled properly is to use a dictionary whenever you are in doubt." A better positioning of words in the sentence might be: "A dictionary can settle any problems of spelling and writing" (or) "To settle any problems of spelling, use a dictionary." If a writer violates the placement principle, the reader's attention may be diverted or lost.

Repetition of essential words or phrases also can be an effective tool for getting across a precise message. Example: "The model B motorcycle is equipped with *sure-contact power brakes;* these *sure-contact power brakes* are responsive to the slightest foot or hand pressure."

Tense

Active voice is far more powerful than passive voice in writing a memo; it gives the impression of importance or urgency. Example of active voice: "The First National Bank of Kingsley, Iowa, now insures your checking account in our bank to a limit of $10,000. The previous limit was $5,000." Example of passive voice: "The amount of insurance to checking account depositors has recently been increased by The First National Bank of Kingsley, Iowa. Before June 15 of this year, individual depositors were insured to a limit of $5,000. The limit has now been raised to $10,000."

Sample Memos

Memo of Instruction

To: Dr. Barbara Nerger
          Chairman of the Psychology Department

From: Elmer J. Passion, Dean

Date: June 1, 19__

Subject: Grade Distribution

I have just finished a review of the grade distribution for the spring semester. I'm sure you recently received, as I did, a copy of this report from the Registrar's Office. I was very surprised to note that the average grade for Psychology was 3.706. That grade average is at least .5 higher than the highest grade average we have in any other department. Given the fact that this is an average for a total of 284 students who took Psychology, this situation raises some concern for me. May I discuss the matter with you when you have time?

Memo of Request

To: Employees of Allied Sporting Equipment

From: Roger Palmer

Date: July 3, 19__

Subject: Travel Plans

To make the most efficient use of employees' travel and time, I will inform the Public Relations Department of trips taken by our employees. Public Relations may wish to ask those of you who are already traveling for other purposes to visit one or two other high schools during your stay. The Public Relations Office has agreed to cover any additional expenses related to your visit at any of these high schools. As soon as you know of your travel plans, please fill out one of the enclosed forms and return it to the Public Relations Department.

Memo of Proposal

To: Physicians of St. Bede's Hospital

From: Director of St. Bede's Hospital

Date: October 1, 19__

Subject: Lighting Fixtures for St. Bede's Hospital

I am enclosing a leaflet for St. Bede's Hospital showing contemporary designs of lighting fixtures by Lipari. Recently, their company was awarded the highest honor in lighting designs for physicians' offices. The choice of all lighting fixtures in physicians' offices at the hospital will be left up to each physician's discretion. The complete line of Lipari lighting fixtures is now on display in their showrooms at 205 Dodge Street, not far from St. Bede's Hospital. However, if you prefer, Lipari, Inc. can have one of their lighting counselors call on you at your office to make a room plan and discuss price and material without obligation.

Memo of Transmittal

To: Board of Directors of Inland Steel

From: Accounting Firm of Bigmore

Date: May 5, 1977

Subject: Financial Report for 1977

Enclosed is the financial report of Inland Steel for 1977. The report is encouraging. The earnings for the fiscal year of 1977 are up 5 percent. If there are any specific questions concerning the report, please contact our offices.

Phone: 341-3890

Address: Accounting Firm of Bigmore
           2700 Main Street
           Waterloo, Iowa

Memo of Inquiry

To: Leonard Drinkmore

From: Margaret Gonzalez

Date: March 5, 19__

Subject: Shipment of Cottage Cheese

On March 3, 19__, we placed an order for 50 pounds of large curd #3 cottage cheese; it was to be packaged in 16-ounce cartons. As of March 5, the order has not yet been received. Please advise when this order was shipped.

Exercises

Write a brief memo for each of the following purposes:

1. To outline a possible problem in a business office of which the supervisor should be aware.
2. To announce a business meeting for plant employees.
3. To outline possible solutions to a problem that will be evaluated at a forthcoming meeting of the board.
4. To inform a colleague that a specific action must be taken before a certain deadline.
5. To pinpoint a target audience for sales representatives of a new product limited to five midwestern states.
6. To establish new routes that representatives of the company will cover beginning with the new fiscal year.
7. To caution members of the firm concerning the dress code.
8. To advise employees not to use the company stationery for private correspondence.
9. To reflect the company's benefit programs for all full-time employees.
10. To indicate potential growth of company if sales are increased 5 percent.

Business Letters 3

Purpose of the Business Letter

You may ask: Why write business letters? Why can't the same information be communicated by telephone or in person? A personal visit with a prospective buyer is not always possible nor is it always the most efficient means of doing business. Long-distance telephone calls may be expensive, especially if the party on the other end of the line must look up records in order to answer a question or if it is a conference call. The business letter, then, is one of the most practical, economical means of doing business.

Detailed and involved information requires written communication. You cannot rely on a telephone conversation or a personal visit to make price adjustments on three different brands of washing machines. These prices changes must be in writing to prevent errors. If your letter is carefully written, it can guarantee accuracy.

Uses

Records

Business letters can form part of a company's official records that can help with bookkeeping and inventory. Letters can be filed in case there are questions about orders or personnel; this cannot be done with a phone call or a personal visit. Letters can constitute a written contract, especially when only an agreement by letter is involved. This is true when a job offer is made by mail.

Public Relations

The business letter is important for public relations; it can help build goodwill. For instance, establishing goodwill through letters can improve sales or gain the confidence of a new client.

Whenever you write a business letter, it is wise to keep your receiver in mind and foresee his or her reaction to your communication. A little practical psychology will create a favorable image of you and your company. You may never have the opportunity of actually talking with or meeting the persons you are communicating with by letter, but their impressions of you and your business are often formed by the letters they receive.

Parts of a Business Letter

Heading

The letterhead contains the name and address of a firm, together with any logo or trademark and telephone number. Letterheads should be designed by specialists or professionals to ensure a certain distinction and appropriateness.

Dateline

Every business letter should show the month, day of the month, and year (October 6, 1978 or 6 October 1978).

Inside Address

The name and address of the party you are mailing your letter to is referred to as the inside address. Titles of courtesy are important; Mr. James Smith, Keith Johnson, M.D., Mrs. George Schuster, and Ms. Carol Washington. You should give special attention to the spelling of the addressee's name; nothing will annoy the receiver as much as having his or her name misspelled. The following are examples of inside addresses and appropriate salutations.

Eric Springer, M.D.
1514 North Drive
Maryland, Virginia 68312

Dear Dr. Springer:

Director of Personnel
Bell Telephone Co.
1514 Dodge Street
Huntington, West Virginia 78192

Dear Sir or Madam:

Mary Doyle, Ph.D.
Professor of Economics
University of Illinois
Urbana, Illinois 96821

Dear Dr. Doyle:

Roberts Dairy Co.
125 Snow Ave.
Council Bluffs, Iowa 34167

Gentlemen:

Mr. Ronald Haskins, Pres.
United Steel and Bridge Co.
1331 South Maple
Peoria, Illinois 96405

Dear Mr. Haskins:

Salutation

The greeting given to the person to whom you are addressing the business letter is called a salutation. Normally, the salutation is typed two spaces below the inside address. It may be formal or informal, depending on how well you know the person. Usually, business letters are formal, and the salutation for Mr. John Smith would be *Dear Mr. Smith:* (A colon is used at the end of a formal salutation.). On the other hand, if the party is a long-time friend, you might say, *Dear John,* (A comma is used to indicate a degree of informality.).

Body

The message of a business letter is contained in the body. Usually, all business letters are typed single-spaced. There is a double spacing, however, between the salutation and the body of the letter.

Complimentary Close

The complimentary close is the formal ending of the letter; it should match the salutation in its degree of formality. You should close a business letter with a friendly, personal remark or an expression of appreciation. For example, one might say:

1. I look forward to seeing you at next month's regional meeting.
2. Please convey my greetings to your partner.
3. If you come to West Bend, please give me a call.

If there is any doubt that a certain complimentary close might be out of place, use the conventional form, "With every best wish" or "Trusting that this letter finds you in good health, I remain."

The complimentary close is usually typed two spaces below the last line of the body of the letter.

Signature

The signature consists of the signature of the writer of the letter with the name and title typed below it. There is a double space between the complimentary close and the signature. The most common words used with the signature are: Sincerely, Sincerely yours, Respectfully yours, and Yours truly. If two words are used for the final words in a letter, the second is never capitalized.

Stenographic Reference

The purpose of the stenographic initials or reference is to identify the typist and the party dictating the letter. In the example below, the initials JCB refer to James C. Birdwell and the 3c refers to a certain typist. The following is an example of how it would appear in an actual business letter using block style.

Hoping to hear from you in the near future concerning the renewal of your insurance policy (2891-A), I remain

Sincerely,

James C. Birdwell
Security Insurance Co.

JCB/3c
Enclosure: 1

Envelope Address

The envelope address should match the inside address of the letter.

Postscript

Postscripts or the "P.S." initials are not used in business letters because afterthoughts indicate a disorganized and casual writer. The expert writer organizes his or her message well to achieve a desired effect. Postscripts may be fine in a letter to a close friend, but they are unprofessional in a business letter.

Layout of the Letter

Block Layout

The block format has no indentation of paragraphs. Two line spaces are used to separate paragraphs. The date, inside address, salutation, body, complimentary close, and stenographic reference begin flush with the left-hand margin of the page.

Semiblock Layout

The semiblock format is like the block format, except that the paragraphs are indented five spaces; the date and signature end at the right-hand margin of the page, and the inside address, salutation, and stenographic reference are flush with the left-hand margin.

Semiblock
Letterhead
Date
Inside Address
Salutation
Body
Complimentary Close
Signature Block
Stenographic Reference

Block
Letterhead
Date
Inside Address
Salutation
Body
Complimentary Close
Signature Block
Stenographic Reference

Style

Language

There is no special language for the business letter, but if you write simply, vividly, and straight to the point, then your letters will be effective. Nothing hurts the style in a business letter more than artificial or stereotyped expressions. Do not write "fully cognizant of" when you mean "aware," or "hold in abeyance" when you mean "stop" or "delay." Concentrate on nouns and verbs; avoid artificial intensifiers such as "very" and "extremely." Unlike fiction writers such as John Steinbeck or Truman Capote, who have an identifiable personal style, your style as a writer of business letters should be inconspicuous, yet indicative of your own unique personality.

Pronouns

Pronouns should not be used excessively in the business letter. Too many "I's" and "we's" make the writer appear self-important. If these pronouns must be used, then they should rarely appear at the beginning of sentences or paragraphs. On the other hand, the pronouns "I" and "we" can give a warmth to your message, for instance, "I'm proud of the fine work you have done in sales." The pronoun "you" can also add a human dimension to your letter.

The Personal Touch

Large companies are often accused of being insensitive in their business correspondence. If you belong to such a company, it is important to be sympathetic and helpful in your business correspondence. One of the best ways to achieve a personalized touch is using the person's name at least once in either the body or the complimentary close of the letter. Another way of adding a personal tone is by sending greetings to a wife, husband, or colleague. Reference to hobbies can be effective in giving a personalized tone. In the following example note the mention of (1) the customer's name, Mr. Johnson, (2) the conversational tone (I'll), (3) his hobby, fishing, and (4) a colleague.

Your order is now being processed, and the new line of Maytags should be in your stores by January 1, 1979, Mr. Johnson, but I wanted to send you a confirmation before I left for Jamaica. After a week's vacation I'll drop by to show you some of the fish I caught and discuss how many new Maytags you may wish to stock in the coming months.

Please give my best wishes to Ms. Taborsky.

The point is that if you know the person, don't treat him or her like a stranger by using formal language.

Whatever you can do to avoid sounding as if you were writing a standardized form letter, do it. Adapt your style to the party you are writing to. If you are an architect and your recipient is not, then communicate in lay terms. There is a great need in our day for a personal approach and an informal tone in letter-writing.

If your language is too technical or old-fashioned, your readers will lose interest; they will be confused by your words and phrases before they have an opportunity to see what your main ideas are.

Active Language

Action is what counts in the business world; you must give the reader strong and vivid pictures. Instead of saying "This ad will draw buyers," say "This ad shouts to the customer." If your language creates vivid images and recalls pleasant memories (refreshing, sparkling, tingling), then your letters will be full of life and action. Some words, such as "bad," "good," "great," and "very" have little or no meaning; they should be omitted because the business letter deals with concrete reality.

The passive voice in business letters should be avoided whenever possible; it gives the impression that something you are writing about has already happened. In the following example, the sentence can be vastly improved by changing the verb from passive to active voice. "The reason for the merger of Sunshine Products with United of Kansas City *will be debated* in two weeks by the stockholders." Revision: "The stockholders *will debate* the merger of Sunshine Products with United of Kansas City in two weeks."

Sentences

Sentences in business letters often are shorter than in other types of writing. Too many short sentences in a row, however, will make your style choppy; an occasional short one well placed can set up an idea. Generally, the sentence lengths should be varied. This can be accomplished by avoiding too many simple sentences and by using more compound, complex, and compound-complex sentence structures.

Paragraphs

Paragraphs, like sentences, should be short. Sometimes paragraphs are only one sentence long, especially in the complimentary close. Although topic sentences are not always possible in the business letter because of its brevity, the overall organizational structure must be a primary concern. If a topic sentence is used in a paragraph, it is best placed at the beginning of the paragraph to give a sense of direction to the rest of the paragraph.

Apart from the complimentary close, however, one-sentence paragraphs should be avoided; they indicate a lack of development and concern for the reader.

Beginnings

The opening paragraph should indicate the subject and purpose of the letter. Using a cliché in the beginning of a letter (such as, "We recently received your correspondence . . . ") is likely to cause a mental yawn in your reader. You should avoid this type of dated format; it will only make your letter sound like a standardized form letter copied from a manual printed in the early 1900s.

Body

The style of the body of the letter should be carefully developed in order to indicate a certain structure. Without structure the purpose of the letter will not be clear. Rational sequence helps the reader see a certain pattern.

Endings

The ending of a letter should not be over one or two sentences in length. The overall tone of the ending should indicate goodwill, friendship, and concern.

If the purpose of your letter is to achieve a certain action, then you should specifically mention this in the closing. For example, if you are writing in behalf of a student applying for a scholarship, then mention the title of the scholarship once again at the end of the letter: "I can recommend Sue McDonald without qualification; she would be a worthy candidate for a Howard Mellon Scholarship in Law at the University of Virginia."

Correctness

Neatness

Just as you would not go to an important job interview in greasy jeans, so you should never send off a messy letter. It may hurt your credibility and the confidence others may have in you. The recipient of a business letter immediately forms an impression of you and your company when the letter is first opened. If there are mistakes in typing, many erasures or handwritten corrections, and careless signatures, the effect is ruined, no matter how carefully the letter has been written.

Exactness

Business letters must be accurate. Policy numbers, dates of shipment, and quality and quantity of material must be checked in order to see whether they match the request. If you don't take this care, you can expect additional correspondence, probably from an angry customer.

Clarity

Clarity in a letter is important in order to have the message understood. However, it may not always be the best policy in certain types of business letters, for example, letters about plant lay-offs, labor disputes, or the reorganization of companies. In these instances, ambiguous language is sometimes the most prudent thing to use, especially if the reader doesn't know the background of the situation.

Tone

Positive

If your letter brings good news or you are saying "yes" to a request, let the reader know about it in the first sentence. This procedure is appropriate even if the recipient must be told that the good news or the granting of a request has certain "strings" attached to it. If the person is told about it immediately, then he or she will be more receptive when the "strings" are revealed.

Negative

When you are responding negatively to a request, you should not mention it in the first line of a letter, but only after you have given some reasons for your decision. Let the recipient see what factual study you undertook to arrive at the decision. When you state your decision, do it with tact so that no resentment develops. Avoid expressions like the following: (1) "You claim that we lost your briefcase in Chicago . . . " or (2) "We regret to inform you that your job with United of Omaha will be terminated as of June 1, 1978." Both of these are tactless sentences that should be avoided. Revise the sentences so that they read: (1) "It is disappointing to learn that your briefcase was lost in Chicago . . . " or (2) "Even though your job performance with United of Omaha was rated as excellent, the company's loss of earnings in the third quarter has forced us to lay off 5% of the staff." After you have made the statement, don't spend the rest of the letter apologizing for it.

In all negative correspondence, develop the *you* attitude which puts the reader's interests first. Write your letter to make it as comfortable and nonthreatening for the recipient as possible. Try to get the recipients to retain confidence in themselves, even though the situation appears bleak. For example, say, "I can mail your airline ticket on Friday . . . " instead of, "I cannot mail your airline ticket until Friday . . . ." Put yourself in the place of the person receiving the letter. You must use a little practical psychology and foresee the recipient's reaction to every negative word you write.

Try to develop goodwill in negative correspondence by focusing on constructive aspects of the situation, and include at least some positive note in every negative letter: "Your résumé is impressive, but, after reviewing the job description, I am sorry to report that we cannot hire you."

Never send a letter written in anger; it indicates a lack of sensitivity and maturity. Put all such negative correspondence in your desk for at least a year; it will look insane, probably, after a week. Remember, business letters don't always stay confidential. A letter written in anger will only prompt the recipient to show it to others or even to respond in anger.

Persuasive

In a persuasive letter the first thing to do is to secure attention and interest by indicating how your proposal will solve a problem or benefit the reader. As the letter develops, you should emphasize the benefits to the reader or show how a solution to the problem can be achieved. In order to support your claims, cite tests, examples, or personal testimonies; these will have the net result of proving your statements. At the close of the letter you should recommend precisely what action you want your reader to take. You may even enclose a return envelope to make that action look simple and easy. Example:

You can still order *Town Voice* now and avoid the rate hikes with today's low prices.

Although mailing costs of magazines have risen sharply, so far our rates for *Town Voice* have increased only slightly.

By using our Courtesy Rates, you can save $12 or more. Plus, save more on a long-term subscription! For example, you can save $16 on *Town Voice* if you subscribe for 2 years at the $32 BFW rate (compared to the publisher's $24 annual rate).

Please share this message with your colleagues and give them one of the enclosed courtesy cards for ordering *Town Voice*. I'm sure they will appreciate your thoughtfulness.

Samples of Letters

Inquiry

October 20, 19___

Dr. Marc Stites
540 North Park
Kansas City, Missouri 80645

Dear Dr. Stites:

Recently I heard about your seminar in sales management which you are scheduled to teach in the fall term at UMKC. Since I have a full-time job in sales at St. Joseph, Missouri, I must commute three nights a week. I am wondering whether you would answer the following questions:

1. How many research papers will be required in the course?
2. How many tests will be given?
3. Do the students participate in class discussions or is the course mainly lecture?
4. Could you send me a syllabus?

As my transcript indicates, I am a serious student, and I want to make sure that I will have the proper time to do all the necessary work for your course.

Hoping to hear from you in the near future, I remain

Sincerely,

Joe Miller
90 Endview
St. Joseph, Missouri 40321

Refusal

September 15, 19___

Mr. Ronald Meyer
1680 Flatrod Rd.
Houston, Texas 90176

Dear Mr. Meyer:

Thank you for your application for a credit account at Big Value Stores here in Houston.

As you probably know, the customary policy at Big Value Stores is to obtain information that can serve as a basis for establishing a credit account. Since you moved to Houston, Texas, from Napa, Illinois, only three weeks ago, we have not had sufficient time to obtain the necessary information.

Thanking you for your letter of inquiry, I remain

Respectfully,

Dolores Montoya
Credit Advisor
Big Value Stores
Houston, Texas 90187

Persuasion

December 1, 19__

Michele K. Morrison, Ph.D.
Vice President for Academic Affairs
St. Ambrose College
Davenport, Iowa 69120

Dear Dr. Morrison:

The budget discussions are now under way. I am wondering whether there might be an increase in the Jaytalkers' budget for the next academic year. Presently, the budget of $3,300 is not sufficient to carry out the program that is not only needed but will benefit the overall academic image of St. Ambrose College. What I am proposing is a budget for debate and individual events of $4,000 for the next academic year.

So far this year (October to January), we have won 39 trophies. On hearing of this success perhaps one might conclude that, if the squad is doing so well with the present budget, why should there be an increase?

The rationale for an increase in the debate and individual events budget springs from the fact that the summer workshop is intimately connected with the success of our debate program here. We have accomplished great things in forensics; however, the debate program is still only average. The staff for the summer school workshop in debate must come from our debate squad that represents St. Ambrose at tournaments throughout the year. Every year St. Ambrose needs superior teams in debate to continue our growth in the summer school workshop. An increase in budget to go to major tournaments is necessary to accomplish this for debate.

The debate workshop is a tremendous recruiting device for the college. It was started two years ago; out of the first class of five seniors, four are back here for their first year of work. They are: Dave Dennis, Harlan, Iowa; Tammy Hetrick, New Salem, Iowa; Paul Crawford, Peoria, Illinois; and Carmen Lang of Portland, Oregon.

Trusting that you will carefully review our budget request for the coming year, I remain

Sincerely,

Sidney Goldstein
Director of Forensics
St. Ambrose College
Davenport, Iowa 69120

Complaint

June 15, 19___

Mrs. Anita Berry
General Supermarkets, Inc.
490 River Rd.
Coleman, Alabama 10786

Dear Mrs. Berry:

Thank you for your letter of June 10 expressing concern at the way some of our employees were dressed at our Better Food Company. We are sorry that you were offended and we have taken care of the situation.

As you pointed out in your letter, we are in a food business that is highly visible to the public; the public expects that good taste be used in the attire worn at the offices of Better Food Company.

As a result of your concern, we have issued a summer dress code. We are encouraging attire more appropriate for an office: pantsuits, sport jackets, dresses.

Thanking you for your interest and concern, Mrs. Berry, I remain

Sincerely,

Gerlard Middleton
Personnel Director
Better Food Company
Coleman, Alabama 10768

Compliment

November 13, 19__

Ms. Gloria Backman
405 Dodge Ave.
Olympia, Washington 50498

Dear Gloria,

Your business sales report for the month of October was carefully
written. With information like this, we can care for the needs of our
customers and anticipate inventory demands well in advance. You are an
asset to the company.

Please convey my greetings to your husband, Patrick. With every best
wish, I remain

Sincerely,

Paul N. Harnett
Director of Personnel
Auto-mate Co.
Loveland, Ohio 19042

Information

June 20, 19__

Mr. Jack Morrissey
Savemore Foods
180 Harnold Ave.
Oakland, California 89040

Dear Jack:

Thought you might enjoy the attached clipping from the *World Herald*.
Martha Sullivan is the Savemore spokeswoman, and I believe Savemore
is her sole sponsor. As the article indicates, she has been around the
market for a long time; she dates back to the Truman era. I know I mentioned Martha and her program at lunch when you were visiting us.

I don't know how many of your divisions have a designated spokeswoman or advertising vehicle on television, but this could be a good way
to reinforce a store-wide pasta promotion.

If the promotion were keyed around a Columbus Day theme, I really
think that "I Discovered Savemore" could be a very marketable slogan.
Spinoffs, such as, "I Discovered Savemore Value . . . Variety . . .

Savings . . . Selection . . . '' would bring home the versatility and economy of pasta as well as short, positive messages to the customers regarding Savemore in general.

If you need additional material or information, please feel free to give me a call at 341-5470.

Sincerely,

George Gommerman
Director/Manager
Sales Services
Pogge Pasta Co.

Exercises

1. You are the head of a committee arranging for the annual commencement speaker at graduation. You have heard that Buckminster Fuller is speaking at night in a neighboring city on the same day of the graduation at your college. The university is allowing you to offer an honorarium of $3,000. Write Buckminster Fuller a letter inquiring if he can speak at the graduation.
2. One of the customers has recently complained about the smell of a soft drink which she normally purchases at a local store. The store always stores the soft drink in the sunny side of the store. You have discovered that this is the cause of the problem. Write a letter of explanation of the action you are taking in the matter.
3. Page through your local newspaper in the "Help Wanted" section and write a letter of application for a job.
4. You received an incomplete in a course in English. From the departmental secretary, you discover that your final term paper was placed in another professor's box who has been on sabbatical for a year. Write a letter to your English professor, who is now teaching a seminar at Stanford during the summer, and inquire about the possibilities of changing the "I" in the course. Supply details and a note from the English departmental secretary.

Business Reports 4

Strictly defined, the business report is an objective, well-planned presentation of facts and opinion intended to accomplish a significant and important purpose related to business. It may be written on one's own initiative or in response to orders from a superior, as we shall explain later.

Just as each person has a unique style and means of communication, so does each group of people. They all have a particular way of relaying information among themselves and to those on whom they are dependent. Medical doctors have, for example, a special way of writing out instructions for nurses and other hospital personnel. In the same manner groups of people associated in the business world use a special means of communication: the business report. It is used by persons of all levels of the business organizational structure, especially management, to give others in their line of work, or those associated with it, the necessary information with which to operate or to make judgments. The business report may move not only horizontally or vertically within an organization, but also outside the business to persons connected with it, such as bankers, lawyers, brokers, or stockholders.

General Content and Purpose

The general purpose of a business report is to give a clear picture of the business so that intelligent decisions may be made. Business reports can be about expansion of plant facilities, decisions about capital funds, pricing of commodities, personnel, the efficiency of day-to-day operations, or even a summary of accomplishments during the preceding year.

The chance of accomplishing your purpose and, thus, of making communication effective is directly related to the quality of your report. Successful management in the business world involves effective communication. The quality, therefore, of the report is also a demonstration of the value and ability of the person who wrote it. Often, the quality of the report is the criterion upon which decisions regarding promotions are based.

By reading the report and studying the visual graphs, management can make intelligent decisions and take prompt action. Since management can't be everywhere at one time, it must keep informed by means of the business report. Carefully prepared business reports can create a climate of flexibility for management; that is, managers can see whether the present policy should be followed or whether some quick adaptation should be made in order to remain competitive.

The specific purpose of a business report can be determined by whether the facts are intended to persuade, inform, or analyze. The persuasive report presents facts that motivate the reader to act or adopt a new opinion. The informational report simply presents facts; the analytic report, on the other hand, besides presenting facts, draws conclusions, makes interpretations, and sometimes recommendations.

Subject

The subject of a business report is usually determined by the department from which it is sent, for instance, accounting, packaging, or transportation. If Chase Candy Company desperately needs five new managers in district plants, the head of personnel might draw up a report for the board of directors describing why five new managers must be hired immediately.

Origin

The origin of a business report depends on a business's needs. Are you, as an employee, required to write the report, or is it a product of your own initiative? Is the report private (originating in a business) or public (originating in government or in some other public institution)? A business report may originate in a department for use within the company or organization or it may stem from a need to inform stockholders or the general public of such things as a program to reduce pollution or a move to hire members of a minority.

Frequency

The frequency of presentation depends on whether the report is issued at intervals or deals only with a particular topic. For instance, Con Agra publishes a quarterly progress report for the stockholders. The American Popcorn Co. occasionally publishes a report on advertising policies, dealing with one particular problem of advertising on television.

Formality

Although business reports are always formal, the degree of formality may vary. The memo incorporates the "To, From, Subject, and Date" format. The letter report uses the body or discussion part to report business. The formal business report differs from a memo or a business letter in detail; its topic is more complex and involved. Also, to make the reading easier, it may often use graphic aids, such as maps, charts, tables, and graphs. It may include other sections for clarity, such as a cover, title page, acknowledgments, table of contents, appendix, bibliography, and index. A letter of transmittal or foreword is also found in a formal report, stating why the report was undertaken. The reader can then place the report within the entire framework of the company. The printed business report may have blank spaces for the writer to fill in specific facts, figures, and statistics.

Prewriting Considerations

Analysis of Purpose

Most business reports are intended to help the reader solve a problem or make a decision. Only by answering questions such as "What is needed," "How can this problem be solved," "Why," and "When," will your report supply the reader with the proper information needed to define the problem or make the proper recommendations. A writer's mind must move constantly from specific data to conclusions and vice versa. To be successful, the process of analysis must begin in the early stages. The more you try to make yourself understood, the better your chance of achieving your purpose in writing the report.

Writing for the Reader

By carefully analyzing your readers, you will be in a good position to determine the way you should write your report. You should not only consider the readers' positions or occupations, but also their prejudices, experience, responsibility, knowledge, and preferences. You must anticipate their viewpoints as customers, stockholders, government officials, or colleagues so that you may influence their decision or opinion. If your audience is a large group of people, such as the board of directors of a bank or of a university, then you might consider whether or not they will be familiar with the subject matter. If, for example, the members of the board of directors are from various professions, it is wise to avoid technical details that may confuse or bore them. On the other hand, if your readers have the same background and are familiar with the technicalities of your subject, you should make a special effort to avoid generalities. In this case, detailed information with facts and figures should be provided to make your material meaningful. Before writing, you should determine precisely what the reader needs to know. To the extent that the reader needs to be satisfied, satisfy him or her. The essence of your report cannot be changed, but the tone, attitude, format, and details can be tailored to fit the reader.

Source Materials

Having determined the audience for the report, you must find sources that will give you the information you need. Technically involved and complex reports may require several sources, while the information for a relatively simple report may be found in company or personal records or files. Secondary data may be obtained from materials compiled in previous similar reports. Using such resources can save time and money. However, a warning is in order: your sources should be checked for credibility and exactness to avoid embarrassment and waste of time. Public and company libraries can be important sources of secondary information. You can also find secondary data in periodicals, books, and government publications. In searching for materials, you should know that many periodicals, books, and government publications soon become dated.

Primary materials are much more difficult to acquire. They are usually unpublished and may require permission to use. You must know your subject well enough to know where you can get information. Company files, journals, minutes of meetings, business letters, results of polls, and personal observations can all be good primary sources. Modern business research uses every method known to scholarship of searching for materials; it conducts surveys, undertakes case studies, and uses computerized questionnaires and polls. The kind of information you need will dictate the type of research you must do.

Organizing the Report

Order of Notes

When all available materials have been researched, the next step is to find an effective order in which to put your notes together. Organization is the best way to achieve clarity. Many writers organize their notes by determining what is relevant while they are researching primary and secondary sources. They write important facts, paraphrases, and quotations on index cards, recording only one item on each card. The cards should then be identified by subject and title and arranged alphabetically in order to tell at a glance what information is recorded on each one. The advantage of using cards is that they can be filed easily; they can be shuffled and reshuffled as your report takes shape.

Be sure to record enough information so that you will be able to write the information accurately in your final report. You need not take complete notes; you may use easily understood abbreviations and contractions to save time. Complicated and detailed reports often require extensive research and time. Material for a short report may be gathered in a few hours, but you must remember that, even in a short report, accuracy is all-important.

Revisions

As you continue to take notes and do the research for your report, chances are that you will have to revise your original outline. Do not hesitate to revise—new facts and information can only improve your final report.

Outline

After you revise your original plan, you may need to construct a final outline. If the report is long and detailed, this will be essential for effective organization. Revising your plan can also prove useful in writing a short report. Your superior may want to see this outline before you start writing the final draft.

To organize an outline, you must be familiar with the general format of the business report. All properly organized reports should have an introduction, body (text), and summary. In other words, you are informing your reader why you undertook the research, what you found in the research, and, finally, what you will do with your findings. Although the introduction appears first in the report, it is probably more practical to write the body of the report first, the summary second, and the introduction third. The body of the report is the most important and longest section.

Introduction

The importance of the introduction cannot be underestimated, even though it is the shortest section in the business report. From reading this section your reader first forms an impression of how precise and clear the report will be. Not all nine points listed below need to be included in every introduction; some may be omitted depending on the subject matter. Introductions usually include: authorization, a statement of the problem, purpose, scope, methodology, background, definition of terms, a statement of results, and plan of presentation. To repeat, you should keep in mind that not every introduction must have all these elements. The nature of your report will dictate which elements should be included. Now let us examine each one of these elements.

Authorization. A statement of authorization is necessary when another person has assigned the report to be undertaken. The authorization can sometimes be stated informally as part of the purpose of the report in this manner: "This report, authorized by (name, title), concerns . . . ."

Authorization to write a report within a company also prevents useless duplication of work. Before undertaking the assignment, it might be wise for the writer to find out who commissioned the report.

Statement of Problem. The problem is an integral part of almost every report. A business report is not like a murder mystery in which important clues are given without revealing the murderer until the end. The essential "clue" in the report must be stated in the beginning. Usually the problem created the need for a report in the first place. Therefore, the problem must be stated clearly and immediately so that the reader knows precisely what you are trying to accomplish.

Purpose. The purpose, too, must be stated clearly and concisely. One simple sentence tells the reader what your work plan will be. You might simply say: "This report is intended to . . . " or "The objective of this report will be to . . . ."

Scope. The scope is the limit of your study, that is, how extensively you have investigated the subject matter. The scope of a long report may include many case studies or interviews, results of surveys, or detailed tables and graphs, whereas the short report may have only a few facts or one case study. For example, a report outlining a pay raise for Lockheed employees will be more intricate and complex than one written for a company with ten employees. In a short report, you do not need to include the scope in the introduction. However, it is imperative that you do so in a long and detailed report. In a longer, formal report you should explain why you decided on this scope and what determined the scope, including information on limitations such as time, money, or available information.

Methodology. In some reports you need to describe the methodology used to collect your information. If a questionnaire (see Appendix A), experiment, or some unusual material is used, it is important to explain these methods in detail because they directly affect the credibility of your findings or suggestions.

Background. Background information regarding the subject matter is sometimes essential to help the readers fully understand the report. For example, stockholders need to know the background of new technology in processing vegetables if the report ends with a recommendation that the company purchase new machinery, costing millions of dollar. You should remember, however, that the major emphasis should be on the outcome or results.

Definition of Terms. Definition of terms is often necessary for readability. If you intend to use a term that has several meanings or one with which the reader may not be familiar, define it. If only a few terms need to be defined, this can be done in the introduction. If several terms unknown to the reader are used, they should be defined as they occur in the text. On the other hand, if a great many words need definition, then you might provide these definitions in a glossary at the end of the text.

Statement of Results. The results should be outlined in the introduction. It is psychologically advantageous to state the results before you discuss the topic. If you think that your report would be enhanced by including your decision, your analysis, or your interpretation of materials, then include it in the introduction. On the other hand, if the materials are such that the results need to be carefully explained, leave the longer explanation until the end. The reason? Including such results in the introduction may only give a false impression or confuse the reader.

Plan of Presentation. A plan of presentation is essential to the organization of your report and its effectiveness. In longer, detailed reports, providing the reader with a statement of your overall organizational pattern will make his or her job easier. This statement should include a summary of the materials you intend to cover in each section of the text. You must make a decision as to what kind of orientation the reader needs to have on the subject matter. Include elements that will improve the readability of the report; omit elements that are not needed or may be handled in the body. If you must incorporate many of these elements into the long report, it may help to divide the introduction into two or more paragraphs, each handling related material of the introductory sections. In the long report subheadings may also be helpful.

Body

Text. The body is referred to as the "text"; but it is never so labeled in a report. Its usual heading is "Data" or "Findings." Since this section of the report is the longest, it should have several subheadings that flag your major points. Even a short report, one having no introduction or formal conclusion, will have the text portion. In reports issued at regular intervals, the text section may constitute the entire report. In the text the readers are provided with the essential details to help them form an opinion on the subject proposed in the introduction. You may include general information to make the topic more understandable, but do not include details. Although such details may be helpful for your understanding, they may be boring or meaningless to the readers. Such information may be itemized in the appendix of the report.

In writing the text of the report, you should include in the first paragraph a brief listing of the points you expect to cover. By doing this, you make sure that the reader understands the overall plan and sees the relationship of one idea to another.

The order in which you enumerate the main points in the first paragraph should be the identical sequence you use to develop the rest of the text. In writing the text, keep in mind that you should present material logically and convincingly to get your reader to agree that the action you propose is the correct one. As you write the report, always keep your purpose in mind, whether it is persuasive, informative, or analytic.

If your main purpose in the report is to inform or analyze, then you will construct the text of the report essentially in the following manner.

1. Cover main ideas or points.
2. Discuss the facts that support each idea.
3. Briefly restate the main points, together with any important conclusions you have drawn about them, especially if your report is an analysis.

If the main purpose of your report is to persuade, then these four steps may be helpful.

1. State the action you propose in order to solve the problem.
2. Explain your proposal with diagrams, charts, or graphic illustrations.
3. Show how your proposal will solve the problem.
4. Give examples and details of how a similar solution to the problem worked in the past (testimony of experts, facts, figures, statistics) or is working in the present.

The organization, language, content, graphic illustrations, and statistical data of the text should be adapted to the needs of the reader. These elements will be discussed later in the chapter.

Style. It is essential to evaluate the needs of your reader. Anticipate the content, organization, language, tone, and general style that will best suit your readers. You would not write a report for the board of directors in the same style as a report for sales representatives or clerical help.

Summary

Methods. Separating the major points into categories of "weaknesses" and "strengths" or "advantages" and "disadvantages" in the summary may be helpful to the reader. In this section you evaluate the facts as objectively as possible. Even though complete freedom from bias is impossible, be careful to draw valid conclusions only from the material contained in the report. New material has no place here. The summary is included whenever a review of pertinent material is helpful. If you make recommendations in the summary, be sure each one is supported by information in the body of the report.

Types. The summary can be a forecast or recommendation as well as a condensation of the major points in the text. The forecast summary tells the reader what will happen; the recommendation summary usually draws objective conclusions on which to base reliable suggestions. These summaries may be titled: "Suggested Course of Action," "Probable Developments," "Advantages," "Forecasts," and "Precautions."

If you suspect that the findings are contrary to the reader's expectations, you may preface your unfavorable remarks with a statement such as "Even though one might have expected oil in Butler County because the scientific analysis looked promising, in the final analysis the results were negative." Try to get your reader to judge you as a believable writer even though the news you have to convey is unfavorable. Finally, list the favorable aspects of a proposition before the unfavorable ones.

In your summary give the reader a sense of completeness and a suggestion about the course of action. Here is an example of a concluding paragraph: "The purpose of this report was to investigate and make recommendations concerning which Philco equipment should be advertised in the fall catalogue. The results of the questionnaire are definitive: 98% of our advertising agents state that market indicators forecast the desirability of full coverage of the Mercury line of TV."

Order

Selecting the order in which to present your information is perhaps the most difficult and important step in writing a business report. The order affects how readable the report is, how easily it is understood, and how effective it is in achieving your purpose. Four of the most common ways of organizing material are: (1) the logical order, (2) the psychological order, (3) the order of importance, and (4) the order of familiarity.

Logical Order

In business reports, the logical order of organizing material is used to persuade the readers to act on a request or to accept conclusions they may not like or expect. When you present your information in a logical order, you are leading the readers point by point through the report until they reach the conclusion or recommendation. If you have presented the facts convincingly and in a logical order, the readers will more easily accept conclusions, recommendations, or requests that you originally suspected they might oppose.

Psychological Order

The second type of arrangement is the psychological order. This is a more direct form: the conclusion is given first, followed by the necessary explanations. This method is effective in long reports in which the readers need a concise summary of the main ideas in order to put the supporting details into proper perspective. The psychologically ordered report keeps the readers from being shocked or surprised by the results. In other words, you let the readers know at the beginning what you intend for them to conclude so that they will have a background upon which to arrange the supporting materials. If you give the readers a pile of complicated facts without giving them your conclusion, the chances are good that they may reach a conclusion different from yours.

The psychological order is achieved by placing the text last, preceded by the summary and then the introduction, or vice versa. Remember, this order is most useful when the readers' only interest is in the material contained in the summary.

Order of Importance

The order of importance is the third way of arranging the report. It is useful in reports involving the description of buildings room by room, factories according to specific function, lands according to productivity, or in any description in which the elements can be ranked.

Order of Familiarity

The fourth method, the order of familiarity, is often used in reports containing complicated material. Difficult material is understandable only if the text is ordered appropriately and explained clearly. For example, you may know that the reader is an electrical engineer who is well acquainted with the type of dam to be constructed. In the report, you must present first the details with which he or she is familiar, and *then* the details that are new or unfamiliar.

Headings

Headings provide immediate orientation for the reader, and they help break up the monotony of one paragraph after another of black type, thus making the report more readable. Effective headings are always brief and to the point and identify the content that follows. Headings in capital letters are more noticeable than those in lowercase letters, just as center-of-the-page headings are more noticeable than those in the margin. In the sentence following the heading, do not refer to the heading by the word "this" or "it." Restate the word or words.

Once you have determined the type of organization to use, you will need to arrange the headings of the major components in the most effective order. The headings should be set up carefully so that you can check the logic of your order for any overlapping or needless repetition.

Headings are basically of three kinds, depending on the tone you wish to set. The kind decided upon should be maintained throughout the report.

Topic Heading

The topic heading most commonly used consists of a single word or a few words, not a sentence. Example: "War on Poverty."

Sentence Heading

The sentence heading is a unit of expression that may stand alone, containing at least a subject and a predicate. Example: "The Great Deluge of '78 Causes Flood."

Variant Heading

The variant heading is a sentence fragment. It begins with a predicate and drops the subject. Example: "Doing Dad Fuller's Way."

Illustrations

The readability of the written report may be increased by the use of illustrations. Illustrations should be near the place of reference to clarify the text. Even though illustrations can make a report look more professional, they should be useful, not just decorative.

You may use many kinds of illustrations, or visual aids, in a business report, such as graphs, charts, tables, and drawings. Before deciding what kind of visual aid to use, you must have a clear and concise idea of what the data mean and what point the illustrations are to focus on. All these visual aids have a specific function and purpose, but some are more useful than others in making a certain point. You should not rely on some favorite type of chart or graph if it doesn't fit the text.

Graphs

Graphs are more interesting and effective than tables but less accurate. One of the main advantages of including graphs is that the reader can notice trends, movements, or cycles much more easily. They are also more concise and revealing. Graphs can condense a large body of information into a relatively small space. How something may be comprehended more easily by a graph is made clear by the following sentence: "The cost of tuition rose 10% during 1977, 6% in 1975, and 4% in 1974." If these facts were put on a graph or chart, the reader could see at a glance the differences in rising tuition costs.

Line Graph. The line graph is used to indicate how one kind of information relates to some other kind. It is drawn by joining a series of points with a line. (See Figures 4.1 and 4.2.)

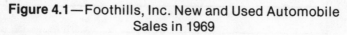

Figure 4.1—Foothills, Inc. New and Used Automobile Sales in 1969

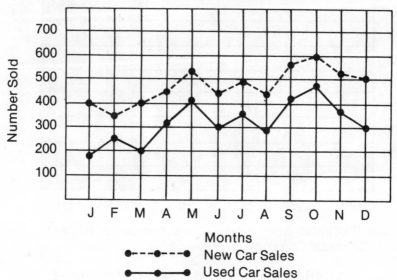

This line graph compares the number of new and used automobile sales at Foothills Imports, Inc.   1969.

Figure 4.2—Home Building Is on the Rise in Weylon County

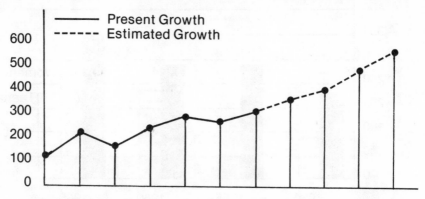

Line graph illustrating the present and estimated home-building trends in Weylon County.

Figure 4.3—Number of Employees Increases as
A & G Chemical Company Expands

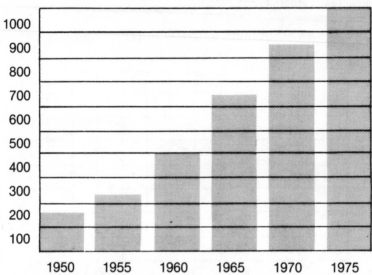

Bar graph illustrates an increase in the number of employees in the A & G Chemical Company.

Figure 4.4—Employee Distribution at Southmore
Electric Company, Inc.

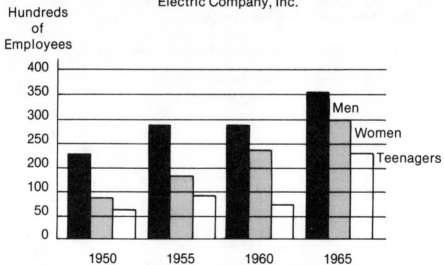

Example of a grouped-column bar graph. Dates are listed along the bottom of the graph and hundreds of employees are shown on the left side of the graph.

Bar Graph. The bar graph consists of horizontal bars crossing the face of the chart from left to right. The bar graph is used to indicate the varying quantities of an item over a certain time period or from place to place. (See Figure 4.3.)

Column Bar Graph. A column bar graph features a row of columns rising from the base of a chart. The tops of the columns are like the line or curve of a line chart. (See Figure 4.4.)

Pie Chart. A pie chart consists of a circle cut into slices like the slices of a pie. Pie charts are useful in comparing changes from time to time or a sequence of totals of different size. (See Figure 4.5.)

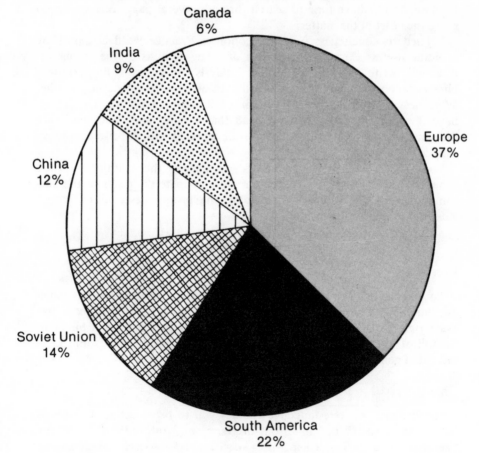

Figure 4.5—Barley Exports to Foreign Nations—1968

Pie chart showing U.S. exports to foreign countries.

Bibliography

If you quote several sources in your report, it may be wise to include a bibliography. In addition to thoroughness, it allows readers to check the sources for more information related to the topic.

Qualities of the Well-Written Report

Conciseness, Word Economy, and Completeness

Your report will be concise if you revise it several times to cut out all copy that does not directly support your ideas. This means that you may have to delete research that took several weeks to complete. People in business do not have time to search through several pages of a report to get to the heart of the matter.

Related to conciseness is word economy. Practice word economy by avoiding useless expressions. Instead of "The analysis of the graphs indicates," write simply, "Graphic analysis indicates." Prepositional phrases take up time and space and should be avoided whenever possible. Wordiness is probably one of the major flaws in report writing. If you have the idea embedded in your head that "long" and "excellent" are the same, forget it. Wordiness cannot be equated with conciseness; long-winded reports should be revised.

Your report will be complete if you answer the questions: Who? What? When? Where? Why? You should anticipate the needs of the person requesting the report by including the proper descriptions, visual aids, and evidence.

Specific and Concrete Words

Expressions

To be specific, you must avoid abstract and general expressions, such as "humanity," "good," "bad," "several," and "few." Instead, use exact figures: "Five percent (5%) of the wheat suffered angel blight in the fall of 1978." The business world deals with specific words and facts instead of generalizations.

Objectivity

Specific and concrete language enables you to be objective. Use terms like "1000 bushels" or "in 75 out of 100 cases," rather than "a lot" or "several times." To repeat, use specific and concrete language to describe reality. The word "defective" is too general to use. If used in a report on automobiles, the word could mean that the auto is completely broken down or it could mean that the bearings in the front wheel are worn out. Be certain that the words used conform to the real world.

You can establish objectivity in the business report by offering adequate proof to support your arguments. Avoid inferences that are not backed up by hard evidence. You should avoid not only false inferences but also value judgments that are not supported by sound reasoning or that are not within the scope of your professional expertise. Inferences and value judgments need to be carefully used and supported by facts.

Emotional language in a business report destroys objectivity; it gives the report too much of a personal tone and indicates opinion rather than fact.

Clarity

Topic Sentence. The clarity of a report can be increased by the use of a topic sentence in each paragraph. A topic sentence states the main idea of a paragraph; the rest of the paragraph supports and develops this main idea. However, the topic sentence does not always need to be the first in a paragraph. Introductory paragraphs in a report have the same purpose in a long report as a topic sentence. The topic sentence should forecast the content of a paragraph. There should be nothing in the paragraph that doesn't relate to this topic sentence.

Transitional Devices. Transitional words like "furthermore" and "moreover" can link sentences and paragraphs. Certain words and phrases act as transitional devices by making the reader look forward or backward. An example of inviting the reader to look backward is this: "From *these figures* we must conclude that the price of wheat will fall 1/10 of one percent in the next week." An example of a transitional sentence prompting the reader to look forward is: "The following statistical evidence indicates how prices on new cars will increase by $250.00 in 1979."

Some transitional sentences can perform a dual task by tying together preceding sentences with those that follow as we see in the next examples: "As we have seen, where two methods of producing methane gas from cow manure have failed to work, the third method looks more promising" or "Not only is the coal miner getting higher wages in 1978 than in 1976, but also his health and insurance benefits are greater." This statement leads the reader to expect that the next sentence or paragraph will go into the insurance and health benefits of miners in 1978.

Illustrations. Reports can be difficult to read if the figures listed are put in the regular text instead of in columns. Example:

TO: Chris Kliesen
FROM: Greg Martin, Treasurer
SUBJECT: Treasurer's Savings Analysis Report
DATE: March 15, 1979

The following statements provide an analysis of the number and balances of the Chicago Savings and Loan accounts in groups of $1,500 for the month of January, 1979. These accounts reflect the period of January 1 and 2 and indicate balances at the Chicago Savings and Loan on these dates.

Total savings accounts were 4,293 with balances of approximately $19,800,000. The average account balance for savings is $2,300.

A gain of 444 accounts has been recorded since the July, 1978 analysis for an increase of 8.97%. Account holders with balances of $4,890 or more make up 34.67% of our depositors. These depositors hold 91.42% of the Chicago Savings and Loan total savings dollars. Depositors with balances of $12,000 and over make up 14.32% of our total account holders, and they hold 49.32% of the total dollar value. This compares with 32.89% of one year ago for an increment of 2.75%.

This report can be improved by putting figures in columns:

TO: Chris Kliesen
FROM: Greg Martin, Treasurer
SUBJECT: Treasurer's Savings Analysis Report
DATE: March 15, 1979

The following statements provide an analysis of the number and balances of the Chicago Savings and Loan accounts in groups of $1,500 for the month of January, 1979. These accounts reflect the period of January 1 and 2 and indicate balances at the Chicago Savings and Loan on these dates.

Comparisons by Number of Accounts and Percentages
Total number of savings accounts 4,293
Gain of accounts since July 1978 444
Increase in number of accounts 8.97%
Depositors with account balance of $4,890 . . . . 34.67%

Comparisons by Dollar Balances
Total balances of all 4,293 savings accounts $19,800,000
Average account balance for all classes of saving. $2,300

Correctness

Tone. Impressions are important. If you wish to make a certain impression, you must fit your "way" to the "way" of the reader. Often the tone established by the writer in the opening paragraph will be maintained by the reader throughout and retained after reading the report. This will be the case, no matter what explanations are given in the text. The overall tone of a report should be persuasive and positive, even when some portions of the report might be negative. You have to give the impression to the reader that the report is significant and important.

Style. The manner in which you express your thoughts is your style. Some writers insist that the style of a report should be impersonal; however, successful reports always reflect the dynamic personality of the writer. In addition to showing that the writer is competent, the report should reflect authority, simplicity, and honesty. When it is picked up and flipped through for the first time, the reader should get a positive impression.

Neatness. Your report must be neat and exact. It must be free of typographical errors. Any such mistake distracts and annoys the reader. Check your report carefully for mistakes in spelling and grammar; every reader becomes a proofreader and critic when it comes to seeing mistakes in the text. A messy report or one with mistakes in spelling and grammar labels the writer as careless, not only in how he or she writes but also in the accuracy of what is written.

See to it that the layout of your report has enough white space; the overall appearance of the report should seem uncrowded. Margins on the left, top, and bottom should be one inch and a half, while the margin on the right should be one inch. Check the length of your paragraphs. Lengthy paragraphs may give the impression that the thought pattern is too complex. A variety of sentence and paragraph lengths will help the overall impression of neatness.

Sample Business Reports

Short Report

Manpower Analysis of the Buena Vista College Speech Faculty

The adoption of a two-hour course, "Communication for the Health Sciences," by the School of Nursing provided the occasion to analyze staffing needs. Ninety-five to one hundred nursing students added to the Fall speech enrollment will greatly increase the work load on our already limited staff. Whether existing faculty can in fact service these additional students, it seems, largely depends on the present and the projected trends for enrollment in Speech classes. In other words, while the addition of a service course for the School of Nursing may not in itself justify hiring an additional person, enrollment in this new course, coupled with an increasing enrollment in all other Speech courses, constitutes ample evidence for additional staff.

Figure 1 demonstrates a clear shift upward in the range of enrollment in Speech classes. Enrollment for next year is expected to range from 250 to 375, while the enrollment for the previous four semesters has ranged from 160 to 220 students. An increase in the number of students taking Speech 151 produced and, we believe, will sustain this upward trend. Figure 2 demonstrates this shift for Speech 151. Enrollment for the coming year is expected to range from 150 to 170 students. Because enrollment in the past seven semesters has been upward, we conclude that additional staff should be hired. Our conclusion is also based on Mr. Oliver Winter's recent appointment at Ryan High School. Apparently, he enjoys his work there and will probably be serving in that position in the future. His departure from our program further reduces our ability to serve Buena Vista students.

Three options merit consideration. First, part-time staff might be added. Part-time staff afford three advantages: (1) they are inexpensive; (2) they are expendable; and (3) they can be hired on a need basis. The disadvantages, however, outweigh the benefits. First, part-time people hinder the coordination of curriculum and departmental policy. This past semester the Speech faculty acted to schedule courses on a regular basis. Table 1 lists these courses and the semesters in which they are to be offered. Part-time faculty tend to complicate and, in some cases, even prevent adherence to a regular schedule of course offerings. Finally, Drs. Western and Williamson concur in the decision to transfer responsibility of the forensics program to whomever is hired. This decision reflects the awareness that forensics is a cocurricular activity that should not compete for time we spend with majors and other students who take our classes. Since a heavy teaching schedule and extensive travel are required of a forensics director, part-time people are unsuited to assume coaching responsibilities. Nor are such part-time people likely to offer a full commitment to the forensics program.

A second possibility is the addition of a person holding a Ph.D. Apart from adding prestige to the department, there would be little advantage, at this time, to hire a person holding a terminal degree. First, such a person would be more costly. Second, a Ph.D. would be on a tenure track and, although enrollment appears to be firm, commitments should be held to a minimum. Finally, a significant portion of the work load assigned to an additional staff member would be in forensics, an activity that does not require a research degree.

The final and favored option would be to hire an M.A. with teaching experience, an option that offers several advantages. First, an M.A. is affordable; one can be hired for around $9,500. Second, an M.A. could be hired as an adjunct faculty member, which would hold the college's commitments to a minimum. Finally, an M.A. would be assigned the forensics program and a number of performance courses that require neither research skills nor an extensive knowledge of the professional literature.

The need to act quickly on this proposal arises from our desire to hire an M.A. with experience. Since contracts are distributed during February and March to the people in whom we are interested, it is important that the decision to hire be made, if possible, within the next thirty days.

Dr. Milton Western

Dr. John Williamson

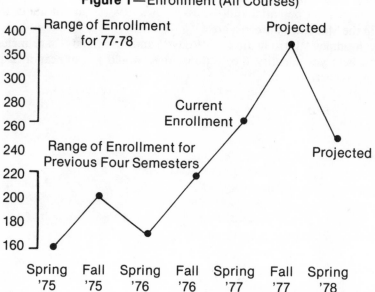

Figure 1—Enrollment (All Courses)

Figure 2—Enrollment (Speech 151)

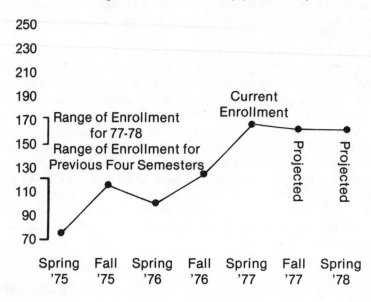

Long Report

The following is a formal business report prepared for a feasibility study explaining in detail the potential of a new restaurant, Wilson's Landing. The report was requested by Western State Bank in order to study the market potential and the assets of a new restaurant about to be built in the Madera, California area.

The headings "Introduction," "Body," and "Summary" are included here to help you identify the sections; they would not appear in a professional report.

WILSON'S LANDING

A Study of Potential and Assets

Prepared for
Mr. Samuel Goldsmith, Manager
Western State Bank
Fresno, California

by

Jim Buttel
Bill's Fish and Chips, Owner

May 30, 1978

(Letter of Transmittal)

May 30, 1978

Mr. Samuel Goldsmith, Manager
Western State Bank
184th and King's Highway
Fresno, California 78132

Dear Mr. Goldsmith:

As you requested, here is my report concerning the potential and assets of the proposed new seafood restaurant to be located in Madera, California.

Throughout the report, I have taken care to be as objective as possible in order to justify the $100,000 which I wish to borrow from your bank at 10% interest. I would like to sign a lease for this new restaurant on July 1, 1978.

If you have any questions concerning my report, I will be happy to come in to discuss them with you.

Sincerely,

Jim Buttel, Owner
Bill's Fish and Chips

Introduction

(The Problem)

The purpose of this report is to outline how my new restaurant, Wilson's Landing in Fig Garden Plaza at Madera, California, will operate and what the initial investment will entail. This information has been gathered to support a loan request from Western State Bank in Fresno, California.

(The Scope)

This report shows the location of Wilson's Landing and the potential market for the restaurant. The net worth of the restaurant is described in detail. Nearly all the data came from interviews with fellow store-owners in Fig Garden Plaza, a study of deeds, past records of Bill's Fish and Chips, and the demographic surveys of the area.

Information concerning management of the restaurant came from my many years of experience as owner and operator of Bill's Fish and Chips. The main source of secondary information was James O'Donnell who has run a similar type of restaurant on the south side of Fresno for the past eight years. The new establishment will be an adaptation of O'Donnell's restaurant.

(Background Information)

Wilson's Landing in the Fig Garden Plaza at 188th and King's Highway in Madera, California, is a refinement of the core principles of my other restaurant, Bill's Fish and Chips. The menu will remain essentially the same, as will the prompt, friendly style. The new name of Wilson's Landing was chosen to make the restaurant's product line and name sound more sophisticated. Although the name is changed, the fundamentals making Bill's Fish and Chips successful in Fresno will still be intact. In an effort to establish continuity between Bill's Fish and Chips and Wilson's Landing, a logo (see Exhibit 1) in abbreviated form will be on menus in both locations as well as incorporated into the interior designs and advertising.

Wilson's Landing is founded on the principles that quality seafood, restaurant-made seafood soups, and a variety of domestic and imported wines are marketable commodities in the Madera area. Five varieties of fish, ranging in price from $1.90 to $3.25, a line of ten different domestic and eight imported wines, and three restaurant-made soups are to be featured. A varied customer profile includes but is not limited to blue-collar workers, clerical and executive white-collar workers, upper- middle-class couples, and an increasing number of high school and early twenties singles. Prior to leasing the premises in Madera, it is evident that, in real-estate terms, the location is a secondary one. The Madera area appears as a strong, unworked market and the location is the only commercial space available in Madera.

The name of Wilson's Landing was chosen for the new restaurant because the name was common and had a native California historical significance: Frank Wilson planted the first vineyard in Madera some 150 years ago.

(Statement of Results)

The intended results of this report will show that a personal loan of $100,000 to Jim Buttel to establish Wilson's Landing is a necessary and a safe investment.

Body

Location Factors

Wilson's Landing at Madera has made a 15-year term lease of 1950 square feet in the Fig Garden Plaza, an excellent neighborhood and trade zone. The attached neighborhood map (see Exhibit 2) delineates Wilson's Landing in black and the lease premises in diagonal lines.

The Fig Garden Plaza has been developed in phases by its owner and developer, The Johnson Company. Each phase was undertaken in response to market demand. The first phase (the building with the courtyard) was developed in 1974. The second phase (the northernmost building) was developed in 1976, and the third phase (the building designated as "proposed" and "future") in 1977. A fourth phase (on the east side of 188th Street) will be started this fall. It will have 16,000 leasable square feet and it is currently 50% preleased.

The neighborhood contains three other smaller centers. The Bluebird Plaza is located immediately south on 188th Street. Another center, Centerdome, is located on the southwest corner of King's Avenue on 188th, and immediately north of it is Brideshead Shopping Center.

Also located in the neighborhood are three large apartment complexes (New Center Towers, Longo Apartments, and Park View Apartments), a townhouse development (Crystalwood Homes), three service stations, St. Gerald's Catholic Church, and several high-quality housing additions (including Britain Towne, The Florentine, August Moon, and Fontenelle Hills).

The topography of this neighborhood features slightly rolling hills. Fig Garden Plaza is at the bottom of a slope. The resulting placement has had no apparent negative effect on the attractiveness of Fig Garden Plaza to tenants or the public. On the contrary, it appears that restaurant tenants are benefitting from the settled, cozy impression caused by its location.

Entrances and exits are by three routes, one major and two minor. The major route is south on 188th Street. Minor routes are north on 188th Street and through the special access road from 189th Street. Even though access is good, it will be improved by the fall of 1977 as street widening of King's Avenue will provide a left-turn bay and light at 189th and King's Avenue.

Total parking spaces available are in excess of seven per 2000 leasable square feet. This is much greater than the recommended minimums of three to four per 2000 leasable square feet. Furthermore, the immediate tenant neighbors of Wilson's Landing are not heavy users of parking, particularly at peak business hours. The area in which parking is congested has been avoided by selecting premises that make it logical and convenient for the customers of Wilson's Landing to use other parking areas.

The tenants presently leasing space in Fig Garden Plaza are shown on Exhibit 3. Phase four will include a day care center, barber shop, and bakery.

Lease Agreement

On July 1, 1978, Wilson's Landing, Inc., a California corporation, wishes to make a lease agreement with The Johnson Company, the owner and developer of the Fig Garden Plaza at 188 and King's Avenue, in Madera, California. The following summary outlines important characteristics of that lease.

Premises

The premises contain approximately 1950 square feet and are located near the north end of the fifth phase in Fig Garden Plaza, addressed as 1905 South 188th Street, Madera, California.

Terms

The primary term is 15 years, with an optional renewal term for 7 years.

Rent

The rent commencement date is December 1, 1978, and the rental for the first 6 months is 5% of gross sales. Rental during the second 6 months is the greater of $733.22 per month or 5% of the gross sales. Rental for the first 12 months is limited to a total of $8,799.66 ($733.22 per month). Rental for each 12-month period thereafter escalates the base amount of $8,799.66 at 2.5% per period.

Interior Improvement Allowance

The landlord is providing an interior improvement allowance in the amount of $12,354 ($6.75 per square foot).

Ownership of Interior Improvements

The tenant owns all interior improvements, except those made with the landlord's interior improvement allowance. Tenant has an express right to place a financing lien on the interior improvements owned by it.

Lease Expenses

The tenant pays its prorata share of the common area expenses and real estate taxes which exceed the base of $ .65 per square foot times the leasable square feet in Fig Garden Plaza. The tenant has protected itself against variables in the tax base ascribable to expansion of the plaza by the landlord.

Use

The tenant is authorized to use the premises for "the operation of a restaurant featuring seafood, soup, and imported and domestic wines."

Parking and Common Area

The lease guarantees the area ratios for parking and common area.

Exclusive

The lease guarantees that no other tenant will be permitted to feature seafoods, soups, and/or wines exclusively.

Rental Abatement

The lease provides for rental abatement upon destruction or condemnation.

Guarantee

The lease is personally guaranteed by Jim Beamer, Walt Jahn, and Lester Goddel.

Market Factors

The characteristics and demographics of the location, which are material to Wilson's Landing, indicate that the market will be considerably stronger than the Fresno market.

The customer profile, which has been developed through the experience of Bill's Fish and Chips in Fresno, indicates that the primary customers of such a seafood restaurant are (1) people in the 20 to 40 age group who have some college education and who are affluent, (2) blue-collar workers, and (3) upper middle class. It is anticipated that Wilson's Landing will find its customers within the same customer profile, but that it will be much stronger among the first and third classifications and slightly weaker in the second classification.

The following demographics for Fig Garden Plaza's trade zone (Marquette to B Street and 150th to 189th Street) compared with the same for the Fresno trade zone (Martha to Billings and 105th to 198th Street) illustrate the positive anticipations for the Fig Garden Plaza.

Demographics	Fig Garden Plaza	Fresno
Total Population	39,370	37,210
Population 20 to 44	37%	40%
Average Household Income	$31,300	$22,897
Per Capita Income	$10,100	$7,130
Disposable Personal Income (per capita)	$8,225	$6,432
White-Collar Workers	45%	40%
Blue-Collar Workers	55%	60%
Some College Education	48%	42%
High School Education	86%	83%

The critical difference between the demographics of the trade zones is in the Disposable Personal Income (DPI). There is 40% more DPI in the trade zone of Fig Garden Plaza than in the trade zone in Fresno. It is reasonable to project this differential into a much stronger classification of customers for both the 20 to 40 age group and the upper middle class.

Other factors that enforce the anticipation of a stronger market at Fig Garden Plaza are the density of the core population and the traffic flow through the routes running adjacent to the center. Because of greater core density, Fig Garden Plaza's primary customers travel less distance and it is less costly to reach them by advertising.

Traffic in the area of Fig Garden Plaza is heavy. The Madera Public Works Department in April 1976 estimated in excess of 27,000 cars per day through 188th and King Avenue. This heavy traffic flow along the boundaries of Fig Garden Plaza brings customers within sight of the restaurant both from the trade zone and from outside the trade zone in a manner which is not available in Fresno.

Competition Factors

There is a need for restaurants in the neighborhood and perhaps in the trade zone of Fig Garden Plaza, and there are no serious competitors in the seafood, soup, and wine field with the characteristics of Wilson's Landing. Furthermore, the location of Wilson's Landing in Fig Garden Plaza and its exclusive rights therein will protect it from competition. The only serious competition for Wilson's Landing would come from other restaurants specializing in quality seafood. At the present time, there are no such seafood restaurants in this trade zone. The closest restaurants are the Sea Shell at 40th and Ames and Lobster Heaven at 90th and Underwood. These restaurants are not in the trade zone of Wilson's Landing; they are not expected to compete for its customers.

The following identifies and discusses characteristics of competition of each restaurant in the neighborhood.

1. Luigi's Pizza Palace is a general competitor. It is the most established restaurant in the neighborhood, specializing in pizza and salads. While it will continue to get its share of the restaurant and carry-out market, it will not be a competitor for the specific market of Wilson's Landing.

2. Mario's is a general competitor. It is a new and successful tablecloth restaurant located in the Fig Garden Plaza. Its broad menu includes steak, chops, salad bar, and liquor. Since it caters to the same and/or similar markets, it could be considered a serious competitor. Its tablecloth and sit-down characteristics, however, are expected to allow Wilson's Landing to serve different meals (seafood) at different times to the same markets and will make Mario's an effective advertising approach for Wilson's Landing rather than a serious competitor.

3. Cliff's House is a minor competitor. It is a fast-food hamburger restaurant with a convenient location and an established clientele. The limited menu, emphasizing fast and inexpensive foods, caters largely to different customers than Wilson's Landing.

4. Wen Den is a minor competitor. It is an oriental food restaurant located in Fig Garden Plaza. A change in management and/or menu could make this restaurant a stronger competitor. Our research indicates that such a change is unlikely but that, if it did take place, it would not cause an interception of the customers of Wilson's Landing.

5. Mister D's is a minor competitor. It is a pizza and salad restaurant with much less presence and position than Mario's. It is not considered likely that it will become a substantive factor in the food-away-from-home or the other markets.

6. Blue Bunny Ices is not a competitor. This specialty store offers ice cream and milk products without a food menu.

Advertising and Merchandising

After extensive experimentation in radio and in newspapers, both weekly and daily, the greatest return for our advertising expenditures lies in advertising in the Madera Sun. A program of consistent institutional ads with occasional promotional ads has proved beneficial as indicated by increased gross sales and new customer count following the introduction of the aforementioned advertising program. Expectations are good for expanding the program with in-house promotions and door-to-door flyers that have proven to be very successful in Fresno (a 7¼% return on 12,000 flyers distributed in May 1977).

Experience to date has indicated that the most successful ads have been (1) informative yet specific and (2) have differentiated Bill's Fish and Chips from ordinary fish-and-chips eateries. Since the ads are, in effect, molding the image of a growing business, returns on advertising expenditures will be residual rather than immediate. At the same time that advertising expenditures have decreased, the gross sales figures have increased. The reasons for this reverse correlation are (1) decreased experimentation in unproductive medias, e.g., radio; (2) consistent use of smaller ads as opposed to periodic large display ads; and (3) careful placement of ads within the media.

Miscellaneous

The following items are considerations of the trade zone, neighborhood, or premises at Fig Garden Plaza that have been underwritten in committing to Fig Garden Plaza as a location for Wilson's Landing.

1. King's Avenue will be widened from 2 lanes to 4 lanes between 150th and 185th Street. In addition to generating greater traffic flow along the perimeter of Fig Garden Plaza, this improvement will cause 189th and King's Avenue to have a left-turn bay and light. The construction period (estimated at 7 months, starting in April or May of 1978) will cause some interruption of the 187th Street access to Fig Garden Plaza. During the construction period, 188th Street will be closed. The closing will be brief, however, and the remaining two access routes will still be open. The insignificance of the access interruption and the constant presence of blue-collar construction workers (an established customer group of Wilson's Landing) during this period have caused us to discount the matter as a serious constraint and to regard it as no worse than a nuisance.

2. "Exclusive Use" rights have been established in the lease, whereby Wilson's Landing has the sole right to feature seafood on its menu. This protects it from interception and other forms of competition in Fig Garden Plaza.

3. "Percentage Rental Only" terms have been established in the lease, whereby Wilson's Landing is obligated to pay as rent only 5% of its gross sales from December 1977 to June 1978, with a maximum monthly ceiling of $733.22. This will permit it to pay rental more in accordance with the value of the location (as measured by gross sales) than would be true with a constant minimum rent based on market rent ($733.22 per month or $5.02 per square foot per year).

Financial Data

The following is a statement of start-up costs to which equity and loan capital will be committed.

1. Professional Fees $1,750.00
   a. Lawyer
   b. Accountant
   c. Architect and/or Graphic Artist

2. Deposits   1,254.00
   (including gas, water, electricity, phones and insurance)
3. Licenses and Permits   275.00
   (including building, health and safety, occupancy, vending)
4. Logo: trademark   300.00
5. Signs   2,000.00
   a. One (1) exterior
   b. Two (2) interior
6. Kitchen Equipment   38,000.00
7. Furniture and Fixtures   9,000.00
   a. Decor
   b. Tables, chairs, booths
   c. Office area
8. Interior Improvements   29,000.00
   a. Electricity
   b. Carpentry
   c. Graphic work
   d. Lighting
   e. Plumbing
   f. Carpeting
9. Inventory (food, tablecloths, dishes)   6,300.00
10. Operating Capital Surplus   10,400.00

Summary

Based on the above analysis, the location, market, and traffic support are ideal for placing in Fig Garden Plaza a restaurant with the product and other characteristics of Wilson's Landing. Although there are apparent constraints from construction work in widening King's Avenue and in the location of Mario's in the same plaza, these are not critical. Furthermore, it is probable that each will neutralize the work or make each one into an advantage.

This is one of the locations in metropolitan Madera with great potential; it will support a successful restaurant for Wilson's Landing. All indications point to the fact that the $100,000 loan by Western State Bank to Jim Buttel to establish the restaurant of Wilson's Landing in Fig Garden Plaza in Madera, California, is a necessary and safe investment.

Exhibit 1

Exhibit 2

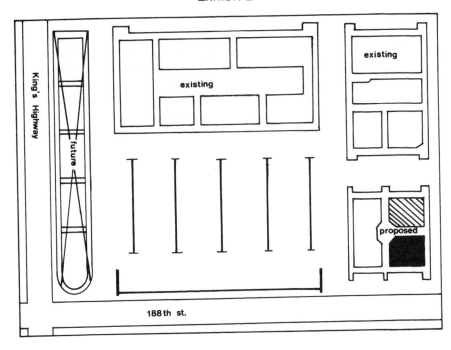

Exhibit 3—Fig Garden Plaza

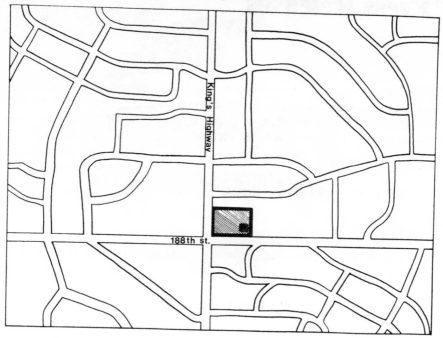

Exercises

1. Imagine that a group of business people in your city want you to set up a Mister Donut in a vacant lot near the local college. Pick out the lot and do a feasibility study.

2. Write a formal report on a project of some company where you have taken on an internship. Make use of secondary sources and at least one kind of primary source. The manager of the company has given you the assignment and topic.

3. The Board of Trustees at State College has hired you to write a report on parking regulations. These are perceived differently by the students and faculty. Write your report, including some graphic analysis, maps, and charts about how the parking may be improved.

4. Write a short report to persuade the president of Hercules Tire Company to increase the advertising budget. Include visual aids that show the increase of the budget over the past five years compared to the increase in sales over the same period.

5. Write a questionnaire that will form the core of a report on employee morale at a local factory. Include questions that will help you analyze the current situation and make recommendations for improving morale.

Press Releases

5

A press release is an announcement of news, accomplishments, findings of a study, or of anything that a company or organization wants the public to know. A good form of public relations, the press release is sent to the media for publication or broadcast.

Traits of a Good Press Release Writer

News Sense

A press release writer must have "news sense." This sense is not so much involved in generating the news as it is in developing an awareness of what will most interest the public.

Motivational Awareness

As a news release writer, you must be aware of the basic motivational appeals that prompt others to think and behave in a certain way. For example, you may discover that one of the professors at your local college is doing some research on muscle contractions. This news may rate a couple lines in the local papers; in fact, there are often similar stories about research projects published daily. However, if you have a nose for news, you will dig deeper for the real story. You may find out that the muscle contraction research really involves how muscle reactions are affected by the intake of alcoholic beverages by giving subjects different amounts of beer and then testing them. The professor may tell you that she is concerned about the number of accidents caused by drunk drivers and that over 1000 students offered to participate in the study when only 100 subjects were needed. This story need not be just an item for the college section of the local paper, but one for the front page, or a story of interest for readers in other parts of the country. The thorough writer always looks below the surface for news.

Public Relations

The Press Family

Even before you write the press release, you should know who will most likely publish or broadcast it. Study the newspapers, listen to the radio news, and watch the television news programs to learn what kinds of stories are included. Then you can write your press release to fit the needs of the local media.

Even though you don't get paid for the press release, it will involve a certain amount of "selling." To market a press release, you not only must be acquainted with the people who will be using it, but also you must know how the newspapers are prc 'uced, printed, and distributed and how the news programs are broadcast. For instance, it makes no sense to send a news release on Tuesday when the newspaper is printed on Monday and distributed on Tuesday.

Poor Public Relations

In dealing with editors and newswriters, you should try to keep on friendly terms, but don't try to buy their favors with too many drinks or luncheons. If a minor misprint or error appears in the story when it is released, don't complain. Remember that the media are highly competitive and operate under pressure. If your press release is omitted, don't angrily call, demanding to know why. You may have to deal with the same people for many years.

Writing the Press Release

Inverted Pyramid Structure

When you write a press release, the most important fact of the story should appear first. In journalism, this order is called the inverted pyramid. The questions Who?, What?, Where?, When?, and How? should be answered in the first paragraph. Details are then developed in the paragraphs that follow so that the busy reader may scan the news quickly. You should also avoid surprise endings; the press release is not like the ending in a murder mystery.

The organizational plan of the press release may be clarified by asking yourself the following questions:

1. What is unique, special, or different about this person or product?
2. Who is likely to be interested in this person, product, or program?
3. What newspapers or magazines should this be sent to?
4. If a program or building is involved, what will it cost?
5. Are the names, dates, and facts in the story correct?
6. Will the story produce any headlines? Striking headlines?

Length of Paragraphs and Press Releases

Modern press releases call for short paragraphs. Such paragraphs help the reader cover the story quickly; they also aid in keeping the interest-flow. Not only should the paragraphs be short, but the entire press release should not be more than one or two pages long. If the press release is concise, it will be more acceptable and readable. Editors or readers don't like to wade through tons of words. Then, too, if the story has to be cut or rewritten, the chances are greater that the original meaning may be changed or distorted.

Style

Perhaps the best style for writing the press release is conversational or journalistic. There is no introduction, development, or conclusion to a press release; hence, it is different from other types of business writing. Your words must interest and inform the reader. Remember, you are not writing the press release to entertain, even though this may happen indirectly. All superlatives, such as "renowned company" or "brilliant insurance executive" should be avoided. Most, if not all, editors will delete them anyway.

Form

The press release should never be handwritten, but always typed, double- or triple-spaced, on white paper 8½ by 11 inches. Your name, address, and phone number should appear on the first page in the upper right-hand corner. This will help the editor in contacting you in case certain points of the news release need to be clarified. Sometimes it is wise to leave the top third of the first page open so that, if the editor or newswriter wishes to include remarks or add a title, there will be room to do it. Leave wide margins on both sides of the page.

Dates

A release date or "For Immediate Release" should appear in the upper right-hand corner on the first page. An embargo is an instruction to the editor that the story should not appear before a certain date. This may prove useful if the announcement of a new official in the company will not be public knowledge before a certain date or if the story involves some timely financial news. Release before the precise date may jeopardize the person or investment involved.

Omissions

Headlines

You should not include any clever, catchy headlines in your release even though it may be tempting. The editors or newscasters won't use them anyway! The same holds true for subheadings.

Underlining

Nothing should be underlined in a press release. Let the editor or newscaster decide what should be emphasized. Underlining to you may mean that the word or phrase should be emphasized, but to a printer it means that the word or phrase should be set in italic type.

Quotation Marks

Quotation marks should be avoided for titles of songs, books, etc.; they should be used only for actual dialogue or when a passage is quoted from another source.

Capital Letters

The careless use of capital letters may cause nightmares for editors; it is best to leave all such "emphasis" up to them. Capital letters should be restricted to proper names and to the beginning of sentences.

Qualities of a Good Picture

Clarity

Pictures are always a big asset to an effective news release. To reproduce well in newsprint, the picture which you include with your story should be clear. Since the newsprint is cheap, the picture should have a good gradation of tone to reproduce well. No editor will publish dull, fuzzy pictures.

Size

The size of the black and white glossy pictures that you mail in with your press release should normally be about 6½ by 4¼ inches. The editor usually has the pictures cropped or blown up, depending on what the particular needs are for the newspaper.

Sending the Pictures

Pictures that are sent through the mail should be backed with cardboard; otherwise, they will arrive crumpled and totally useless to the editor. Pictures should not be stapled or paper-clipped to the press release; this will only damage them. Mars on the print will appear on the pictures when they are published.

Sample Press Releases

George R. Wendt's Press Release

TO: FOR: Immediate Release

                           CONTACT: George R. Wendt
                                       225 North Harrison Street
                                       Batavia, Illinois 60410
                                       Phone: 312—865-2383

The Illinois Association of Professional Insurance Agents, Inc. (IAPIA) announces the appointment as Assistant Executive Director of George Wendt of Batavia. IAPIA is a trade association of over 800 independent insurance agents in Illinois who market property and casualty insurance for homes and automobiles, for commercial properties, and other insurable risks.

Wendt, a 20-year resident of the Fox Valley, holds BA and MA degrees in Economics from the University of Illinois. He has held general and personnel management positions with major companies in the Fox Valley and Chicago suburban areas and is a contributor to several professional journals.

Formerly with the Health Insurance Association of America as a regional director, Wendt has held elected office in various area volunteer and professional groups. He has served on the Batavia Board of Zoning Appeals since 1969. He is an Honorary Member of the Society for the Advancement of Management of Northern Illinois University and is a member of the American Society of Association Executives and the International Platform Association. He serves on the Board of Directors of Playmakers, Inc., a Valley theatrical group. Formerly licensed as an insurance field underwriter, he has taught in the evening programs of both Aurora College, Aurora, and the College of DuPage, Glen Ellyn. He also conducts personal development workshops.

The IAPIA sponsors Certified Insurance Counselor (CIC) quarterly training seminars at the University of Illinois. Written testing following the four seminars leads to the CIC designation. State legislation in Springfield affecting the insurance industry is monitored closely. Additional Association effort centers on insurance agent-insurance company working relationships, other special education for member agents, public relations, finance, member services, and growth. An annual convention is held in the fall. The Association maintains operations from Champaign-Urbana and Batavia.

The IAPIA annual convention concluded recently in Peoria. The annual convention of the National Association of Professional Insurance

(more)

Agents, of which the Illinois Association is a constituent, will convene in Chicago late in October. Agent members of IAPIA will play an important role as the hosting Association for the 1,000 independent agents and wives attending.

The Illinois Association of Professional Insurance Agents is governed by a 15-person Board of Directors and officers. Past presidents of the Association serve as continuing advisors to the Board. Past presidents from the Fox Valley area include Ira C. Johnson of Aurora, John R. Stone of Elgin, and Ellsworth Windett of Yorkville.

(End)

Fr. Matthew E. Creighton's Press Release

TO: FOR: Immediate Release

CONTACT: Maria Vakulskas
2930 California
Omaha, Nebr. 68178
Phone: 204—312-8940

The Rev. Matthew E. Creighton, S.J., 51, director of Research Services and professor of classical studies at Loyola University of Chicago, will become the 21st president of Creighton University effective July 1, 1978.

Father Creighton was appointed by the Board of Directors at their April meeting. The announcement was made by Jack A. MacAllister, chairman of the board.

Father Creighton succeeds the Rev. Joseph J. Labaj, S.J., who announced his resignation last year. Father Labaj will become provincial for the Wisconsin Province of the Society of Jesus effective August 1, 1978.

Father Creighton is a native of Chicago, Ill. He has been director of Loyola's Research Services since September 1976. He was responsible for establishing an expanded physical facility for research services. He developed comprehensive files and tracking systems and strengthened contacts with local, state and federal agencies. At Loyola, he was also academic dean of the Rome Center from 1974-76 where he was responsible for introducing a highly articulated system for making new faculty appointments. The Rome Center is a school in Rome, Italy, operated by Loyola, which serves American students abroad. Father was associate dean of Loyola's Graduate School from 1970-74 and chairman of the Department of Classics from 1968-72.

A 1944 graduate of St. Ignatius College Prep in Chicago and a 1948

(more)

graduate of Milford College of Xavier University in Cincinnati, Father Creighton holds an undergraduate degree in classics and a master's degree in systematic philosophy from Bellarmine College of Loyola University. He also holds a master's degree in classics from Loyola University and a licentiate from the Bellarmine School of Theology of Loyola University. In 1967, he received a doctorate from Fordham University in classics. He also has studied at the universities of Detroit, Michigan, Nebraska, and at Harvard University.

Father Creighton entered the Jesuit order in 1944 and was ordained in 1957. He took his final religious vows with the Jesuits in 1962.

He serves on the faculty of the College of Arts and Sciences and the Graduate School at Loyola.

Father Creighton is the author of four books: A Summary of the History of Greek and Latin Literature, A Computerized Concordance of Tertullian, A Critical Edition of the Complete Works of Decimus Magnus Ausonius and a translation of Galiani, Ferdinando, Della Moneta by Peter R. Toscano. He is also the author of articles on classics and has constructed language learning aids.

Professional memberships include the American Philological Association, American Society of Papyrologists, Association of American Colleges for Teacher Education, Association of Jesuit Colleges and Universities, National Catholic Office for Motion Pictures, where he is a consultant, National Council of University Research Administrators and the National Council on the Teaching of Foreign Languages.

Father is the son of Dr. Matthew and Mrs. Mary Creighton of Chicago. Dr. Creighton was a surgeon and a faculty member of Loyola prior to his death. Other family members include Sister Mary Creighton, I.B.V.M., Grace Creighton and the Rev. James J. Creighton, S.J., all of Chicago, and Robert Creighton, from Philadelphia, Pa. All are educators.

Father Creighton comes to Creighton University during its centennial year of celebration. He is not related to the original founders, brothers John and Edward Creighton and their wives Sarah Emily and Mary Lucretia.

Creighton is a private, Catholic university located in Omaha, Nebraska, with an enrollment of 5,000. The university has undergraduate colleges in arts and sciences, business administration, and nursing; a graduate school; and schools of medicine, law, pharmacy, and dentistry.

(End)

The Sue Bee Squeeze Container Press Release

TO: FOR: Immediate Release

                              CONTACT: Steve Goodman
                                          Sue Bee Corporation
                                          19th & Jackson
                                          Sioux City, Iowa 51390
                                          Phone: 402—341-2542

Honey from Sue Bee Corporation of Sioux City, Iowa is now being packaged in unbreakable plastic squeeze containers attractive enough for any dinner table. This will mean an end to messy knives and spoons, dirty bowls, and wasted honey.

The new plastic squeeze containers are made of hygienic, clear plastic and are disposable when empty. These new plastic containers will end the problem of ants and other pesty insects invading the kitchen because of drippy glass and tin containers.

The Sue Bee plastic containers have attractive floral designs and can be carried in a lunch pail. The opening on the top of the container has a special locking device preventing children from accidentally spilling honey.

Prices on the new honey squeeze containers will remain the same as before at Safeway, Hinky Dinky, and Sunshine Supermarkets.

(End)

Exercises

1. Imagine that you have just finished your final year at Harvard University School of Law in the top five percent of your class. You have just taken a job with Merrill Lynch Co. where you head the Mutual Funds Investment Division in Kansas City, Missouri. Write a press release for the newspapers in Kansas City.
2. Write a press release on a new type of seed corn or grain which you raised on an experimental plot at Michigan State University. The seed corn or grain can be grown in soil that has only an annual rainfall of seven inches. Possibilities are good that it may solve the starvation problems in underdeveloped countries.
3. Write a press release on a stock split for Uni-Royal Tire Co. Point out what this will mean for the stockholders and the future development of the company.

Sales Call Reports 6

The main purpose of management is decision making, and intelligent decision making requires pertinent and useful information. Your sales call report is what will supply the management team of your company with the vital information upon which to base their decisions. Your knowledge and judgment as exhibited in the sales call report are needed to guide others in the company. Your report will influence the company's advertising, trade allowances, pricing, shipping, manufacturing, and virtually every activity of the company. Your reports will be routed from the sales department all the way up the ladder to the chairman of the board.

Sales supervisors, district sales managers, regional sales managers, and directors of sales all write sales call reports. Each will include different types of information for different areas, but the guidelines for writing a good sales call report will be the same.

Preparation for Writing

In preparing to write the sales call report, you don't have to make a formal outline. Write down the topics and key thoughts you wish to cover, keeping in mind the following guidelines: (1) include all important topics, (2) organize your thoughts chronologically or in order of importance, and (3) spend less time writing the report.

Material Included

Descriptive Information

The list of sales information given below is only a partial list of what you will need to include. Remember that no one sales call report can cover all these topics. However, in the course of working several years for a company you will probably cover each one of these topics in your report.

1. Market. What are the competitive brands? Who are the distributors? Who has the largest share of the market? Who is gaining in sales? Who is losing in sales? Why?

2. Brand Name. What is the condition of the company's retail displays? What about rotation? What is the point of the sales material? What is the retail pricing? What are the gains or losses of new items? What is my company's share of the market? What share of the shelf space do the items my company sells have?

3. Competition. Who are the company's competitors? What is the competition doing with regard to pricing, trade allowances, product quality, new products, and advertising?

4. Customers and Potential Customers. Who are the customers and potential customers? What is their annual volume? How many stores do they have; how big are the stores; where are they located; who are the key personnel in each account?

Evaluative Information

1. Broker. How effective is the broker in store merchandising and servicing? What are his or her retail call frequency and coverage? How many retail people does he or she have? Are they well trained? Are they known at the store level? What does the trade think of them? What is the turnover rate for the broker's retail force? What about direct calls? How well does the broker know key customer personnel? How professional are his or her presentations? Can the broker get things done at headquarters?

2. Competition. What is the competition doing that will affect my company? Are the competitive tactics successful or not? What should my company do to counteract competitive tactics? Throughout my area, who is getting stronger and who is getting weaker in sales, and why?

3. Brand Name. Are my company's product, package, price, and shipping service all competitive? Am I given the correct selling and marketing tools?

4. Opportunity. Is the competition selling poorly in an account? Is the profit return to the retailer too low? Is the retail coverage being neglected? What account would be most receptive to my company's presentation? What accounts stock fewer than the average number of my company's products? Does my company have the right product mix? What lines of my company's products are gaining in popularity?

Elements in Writing the Sales Call Report

Judgment

Since you can't report every detail of what is happening in your sales territory, you must use your judgment as to what will make a good report or a poor one. You will write a good report if you consider the person you are writing it for and answer the following questions:

1. What does he or she need to know to do a better job?
2. What does he or she want to know?
3. What do I think is important?

Brevity

A lengthy report on a trivial matter is boring to read and is a waste of time. An incomplete report on an important matter is worse. In general, highlight your topics and use language that is direct and to the point. If, however, you are reporting on a subject that is complex and critical to the company's progress, then take the time to give the full details.

Headlines

The key topics of your sales call report should be headlined for emphasis. Headlining not only makes it easier for the reader to get your message, but it also is a great help in locating a topic you wrote about in a previous report.

Objectivity

You should document all your observations. For example, don't say, "Brand X is advertising very heavily in this market." Instead, report that Brand X is using television and radio. Find out how many weeks and how many times per week it has advertised. If you do this, your company can react in an informed way. When you report that 20 items were placed in Cole King's Supermarket, add the facts that this is a $55,000-per-week store and your company will have 40% of the space.

Exaggeration

Tell it like it is, but don't overemphasize the "I." Since it is your report, you cannot avoid the use of the word "I." However, don't use the sales call report to build up your own accomplishments; the readers up the line will see through this. A job well done will speak for itself.

Correctness

Proofread what you have written. Ask yourself the question, Did I include everything I wanted to say? Are there any mistakes?

Sample Sales Call Report

Lorenzo Spaghetti Company

To: Henry Harrington   Date: October 18, 19__

From: Brice O'Neill   Subject: Sales Call Report
                                               October 9-13, 19__

Monday, October 9
I worked out of my office in Denver in the morning. In the afternoon I dropped off some information for Bill Graves, the buyer at Fort Meyers, concerning new items for the Super-Saver Stores out of Kansas City. I flew to Dallas, Texas, Monday evening and met with Stanley Brady. Stanley and I reviewed the information concerning the Market City call tomorrow morning.

Tuesday, October 10
I made a presentation to Mr. Russ Horning, the Merchandiser Director of eight Market City Stores in Dallas. We presented 33 items and a program for 40% of the space in all eight Market City Stores. This was an excellent call, and all indications are that we are going into the Market City account. Russ Horning wanted us to survey all eight stores and provide information about the number of feet in each store, number of shelves, number of Italian Delight items, and facings. This information will be compiled this week and sent to Mr. Horning on Monday, November 5. The proposal presented to Mr. Horning was basically the same as the proposal presented in July. We updated it with the new prices and added a sheet to give him a total distribution picture of Lorenzo/Italian Delight and other brands in the Dallas market. We also worked up a list of independent stores that he directly competes with and gave him the number of items that Lorenzo carried in each. He should give us a decision on the Lorenzo line next week. After leaving Market City I had a meeting with John Hoffmann at Better Brokerage Company to discuss the handling of damage credits on Lorenzo products at retail. We also discussed our promotion quota on 24 oz. spaghetti and retail coverage of the two Martin West Co. stores in Mississippi: Canton and Natchez.

After leaving Better Brokerage Company, I made retail store checks with Bill Lynch. All stores we checked were in good shape. Departments were full and well merchandised, and they are making good use of recipes and point-of-sale material.

Wednesday, October 11
Carl Lo Sasso, Bill Goodman, and I continued to make store checks

throughout the Dallas market. I was pleased with the results of our check. The retail salespersons in Dallas seem to be doing a very good job on our Lorenzo products. Bill Goodman will be forwarding a retail store check report concerning the calls made until now. I left Dallas Wednesday evening and returned to Denver.

Thursday, October 12

I worked out of my office in Denver, taking care of mail and working on some military information for a Fort Meyers call the week of November 13. We are going to be representing this base to reinstate the Lorenzo line. They have a new commissary officer, Mr. Larry Jelinek.

Mr. Jelinek's other commissary duties were at Fort Washington and Fort Bennington. He is unfamiliar with the Lorenzo line. He is currently on leave from Fort Cody and will return Monday, October 23, at which time I will contact him to set up an appointment for a full presentation. We are also working on a project for a demonstrator to hand out 9¢-off coupons on the Lorenzo line at Johnson A.F.B. The commissary officer at Johnson A.F.B. has agreed to a 425-case display on three items: 180 (24 oz.) thin spaghetti, 20 (24 oz.) short cut, 225 (12 oz.) thick cut. This display will be in support of the in-store demonstrator handing out 3,500 9¢-off coupons. The coupons will be good on any Lorenzo Spaghetti product and we will work the entire department, but the display will support the extra purchases in our product line. We are currently targeting the first of November for this demonstration. After Johnson A.F.B. we plan to use the same program at Murry A.F.B. These two demonstrator coupon programs should help combat the heavy advertisement by the Marco Co. in bases here in Colorado. The commissary officer at Johnson, Bob Reilly, says that it looks as if all Colorado A.F.B.s will be merged under Johnson A.F.B. The bases under this complex at Johnson A.F.B. will be Beaudrow, Warren, and Henderson. We should know more on this in the next 30 days.

Friday, October 13

I worked out of my office Friday morning. In the afternoon I met with Patricia Wolfe for a brief time to pick up the copies of Randy Andy plan-o-grams and to review key accounts in Colorado. Pat Wolfe is doing an excellent job of communicating with area merchandisers in Colorado. We are building a strong sales force in Colorado under her supervision. I am currently channeling most of her efforts in Colorado to help rebuild our distribution, including the A.F.B. stores. She is doing a good job in this area. I plan to bring Leroy Jones over to the Colorado market within the next two weeks and channel most of his immediate efforts at working directly with our retail stores. By doing this, he will get a better feel of our market and the accounts that we cover and develop a better

understanding of the weaknesses and strengths of the various area merchandisers he works with.

Exercises

1. Keep a journal of what you do every day for a week. Mention how
    you spend your time, the work you do, the people you talk with, and
    what you talk about.
2. You are an advertising sales person for the college newspaper. Make
    out a weekly report of the prospects you contacted, their reactions,
    and how you are attempting to get new accounts.
3. You are a sales representative for a growing publishing company.
    Because your territory covers the entire East Coast, you make over 20
    calls a week on bookstores. Write a sales report of a typical week's
    work.

Appendix

The following is a questionnaire sent by the Subcommittee for Educational Research and Development to the faculty of the College of Liberal Arts at William and Mary College to evaluate Program 101.

Faculty Opinion Survey
Subcommittee for Educational Research and Development
Program 101 Evaluation

August 15, 1978

Please return this questionnaire to Social Science Data Lab, Room 424, Administration Building by August 25, 1978.

1. All faculty members of the College of Arts and Sciences were invited to apply to participate in Program 101.
   (a) Did you apply to participate? ☐ Yes
                                       ☐ No

   If yes, for which year(s)? _____
   (b) Would you please tell us what influenced you in your decision to apply or not to apply.

   _____

   (c) Did you eventually participate? ☐ Yes
                                         ☐ No (skip to e below)

   If yes, for which academic year(s)? _____
   (d) If you did participate, would you consider participating again? ☐ Yes
                                                                         ☐ No

   Why would you consider/not consider participating again? _____

   _____

   (e) If you have never participated, would you explain why, and what changes in Program 101, if any, might encourage you to want to participate?

   _____

   _____

2. Would you please indicate whether or not you are familiar with the following programs, and whether or not you have applied to participate in any of them.

78

	No, not familiar	Yes, I am familiar but have not applied
C.E.C.	☐	☐
Honors Program	☐	☐
Independent Study	☐	☐
Internships/Externships	☐	☐

3. Every program has some features that are considered good and some bad. What do you believe are the three best features about Program 101 as it now operates?

   (a) _____

   (b) _____

   (c) _____

   What do you believe are the three worst features of Program 101 as it now operates?

   (a) _____

   (b) _____

   (c) _____

4. If the decision were strictly yours, would you continue Program 101 in its present form? ☐ Yes
   ☐ No

   If no, can you suggest changes in the program that would merit its continuation?

   _____

5. Would you advise a freshman student to enroll in Program 101? ☐ Yes
   ☐ No

   Why?_____

6. If a colleague were considering participating in Program 101, would you advise him or her to do so? ☐ Yes
   ☐ No

   Why?_____

7. (a) Do you think there are any benefits for the student in Program 101 that are not available elsewhere in the Arts college? ☐ Yes
   ☐ No

   If yes, what are those benefits? _____

(b) Do you think there are any benefits for the faculty member who participates in Program 101 that are not available elsewhere in the Arts college?   ☐ Yes
   ☐ No

If so, what are those benefits?_____

8. (a) Do you think there are any risks for a student in Program 101 that are not encountered elsewhere in the Arts college?   ☐ Yes
   ☐ No

If yes, what are those risks?_____

(b) Do you think there are any risks for the faculty in Program 101 that are not encountered elsewhere in the Arts college?   ☐ Yes
   ☐ No

If yes, what are those risks?_____

9. Do you have any other comments to make about Program 101?

LANGUAGE ARTS BOOKS

Speech
Person-to-Person, Galvin and Book — 5202-8
Person-to-Person Workbook, Galvin and Book — 5202-7
Speaking by Doing, Buys — 5025-2
Adventures in the Looking-Glass, Ratliffe and Herman — 5208-5
Oral Interpretation, Gamble and Gamble — 5107-0
Contemporary Speech, HopKins and Whitaker — 5204-2

Media
Understanding Mass Media, Schrank — 5226-3
Understanding the Film, Johnson and Bone — 5037-6
Photography in Focus, Jacobs and Kokrda — 5414-2
Televising Your Message, Mitchell — 5011-2

Theatre
Play Production in the High School, Beck et al. — 5101-1
The Dynamics of Acting, Snyder — 5106-2
Acting and Directing, Grandstaff — 5115-1
Stagecraft, Beck — 5104-6
An Introduction to Theatre and Drama, Cassady and Cassady — 5102-8

Mystery and Science Fiction Literature
The Detective Story, Schwartz — 5608-0
You and Science Fiction, Hollister — 5555-6

Business Communication
Successful Business Writing, Sitzmann — 5230-8
Successful Interviewing, Sitzmann and Garcia — 5229-8
Working in Groups, Stech and Ratliffe — 5145-3

Grammar
The Great American Grammar Machine Vol. 1, Pratt — 5500-2
The Great American Grammar Machine Vol. 2, Pratt — 5500-4

Writing and Composition
Snap, Crackle & Write, Schrank — 5235-2
Journalism Today!, Ferguson and Patten — 5208-4
An Anthology for Young Writers, Meredith — 5604-8
Writing in Action, Meredith — 5605-6

Tandem: Language in Action Series
Point/Counterpoint, Dufour and Strauss — 5248-4
Action/Interaction, Dufour and Strauss — 5249-2

Teacher's Editions, Workbooks, Testing and Evaluation Spirit Masters, and Student Record Profiles available.

 NATIONAL TEXTBOOK COMPANY • *Skokie, Illinois 60077*